Alas, Alas for England

LOUIS HEREN

Alas, Alas for England

What Went Wrong with Britain

> But they that fought for England,
> Following a falling star,
> Alas, alas for England,
> They have their graves afar.
>
> And they that rule in England,
> In stately conclave met,
> Alas, alas for England
> They have no graves as yet.
>
> G. K. CHESTERTON

HAMISH HAMILTON

LONDON

First published in Great Britain 1981
by Hamish Hamilton Ltd
Garden House 57–59 Long Acre London WC2E 9JZ

Copyright © 1981 by Louis Heren

British Library Cataloguing in Publication Data

Heren, Louis
  Alas, alas for England.
  1. Great Britain – Politics and
  government – 1945–
  I. Title
  941.085   DA588
  ISBN 0–241–10538–2

Typeset, printed and bound in Great Britain
by Redwood Burn Ltd, Trowbridge and Esher

Contents

Foreword

Donald Tyerman once said that I knew all about the springs of American power and policy, but little or nothing about the British equivalent. He might have added that at various times I also knew more about the Middle East, the Indian sub-continent, Southeast Asia and Western Europe than Britain, and that he was largely responsible.

Donald had promoted me to foreign correspondent when he was deputy editor of *The Times* and over the years the land of my birth had gradually become almost a foreign country.

I eventually came in from the cold and found the natives still friendly but their ways mysterious. The mystery deepened as the country's decline grew more disturbing and puzzling. I could not understand why the British, a talented, inventive and imaginative people, could not do better for themselves, and finally decided to take Donald's implied advice and find out why.

I approached the task as a foreign correspondent, which basically means asking obvious questions, reading and travelling widely and, above all, working with the objectivity which foreign correspondents can develop because they live in societies without being part of them. That was not easy although I had spent most of my adult years abroad. Memory and atavism obtruded as did, I suppose, a protective loyalty to my own kind, but at least I saw them with fresh eyes. There were some surprises. Men and women in many walks of life were eager to talk, most of them on the record, and some were no less disturbed and puzzled. I have not quoted all of them, but I thank them for their confidence and cooperation.

I must also thank Cathy James who helped organize the enquiry and typed and corrected the manuscript.

L. H.

ONE

Wider Still and Wider. . .

This is one man's view of Britain in decline, and a short biographical note is probably necessary. I do not claim to be objective; indeed, after a lifetime in journalism I am instantly suspicious of any writer or politician who claims that elusive quality. The perception of any situation depends upon the background, ambitions, limitations and prejudices of the beholder; hence the need for a biographical sketch. I was born in London's East End during the Depression, and went to work when I was fifteen. I shared the aspirations of the new Labour government when I was mustered out of the army after the second world war. I welcomed the foundation of the welfare state, and assumed that Britain would become a happier and more egalitarian society. As a foreign correspondent of *The Times*, I reported with satisfaction the dissolution of the British Empire; in part because I believed in the rights of man, including the right to rule or misrule himself, but mainly because I wanted a new beginning. I really believed that once rid of the burden of the past the ordinary people of this country, of whom I was one, could make a go of it.

Some readers are perhaps anticipating an admission of disillusion. Others might think that this is to be another doom book. I hope that both will be proved wrong. Obviously the earlier hopes of my generation have not been realized. I am disappointed, but no more than that because I do not believe in Utopias or the perfectibility of man. Moreover, for the vast majority of the population in many ways life is much better than when I was a boy. They are better fed and housed. Their horizons have been widened by television, radio and newspapers, by motor cars and packaged tours. Higher education is more readily available for their children, and the National Health Service, for all its faults, has improved health and reduced some of the terrors of pain and ageing. Disappointment came slowly perhaps because I spent little time at home or in Europe during the early post-war years. Then I was posted to Bonn in the mid-fifties, and before the end of the decade became uneasily aware that Britain was doing less well than other modern industrial democracies. The impressive progress of West Germany and other western European democracies underlined the decline of Britain.

It is true that in relative terms the economic decline of Britain had been obvious for years, certainly long before the first world war. I was also aware of the great damage that that war had done to the country. I grew up in its aftermath, a period of deprivation and desolation made worse by the selfishness, stupidity and short-sightedness of those who governed us. This might lead some readers to ask why I confined my enquiries to after the 1939–45 war. One reason is that I am a journalist and not a historian, but there is more to it than that. The second world war was a great watershed. The British people emerged from their heroic struggle with great self-confidence. We were well placed to take full advantage of the unprecedented period of economic expansion that quickly followed. We could and should have made a go of it, but we missed or fumbled many of the opportunities. We largely failed to adjust to a changing world. The decline continued, apparently inexorable by the mid-seventies, and much of it can be explained by what was done and not done after the war.

Other readers, remembering the post-war increase in living standards, will perhaps reject the assumption that Britain is in a state of decline. They might agree with Bernard Nossiter, who argued in his book *Britain; A Future That Works** that the condition of Britain was the consequence of the conscious choice of the majority. He believed that Britons were the first citizens of the post-industrial age to choose leisure rather than material goods. The relatively slow economic growth was not the result of an excessive welfare or tax burden, the dismal product of any equalizing of incomes, or the penalty imposed by militant leftist unions or a bitter class struggle; it reflected an attitude, a life style, a choice. Britain was a society more or less at peace with itself, generally orderly, generally tolerant, more or less humane.

Nossiter would have been more persuasive had he written earlier; say in 1966 when *Time* magazine discovered swinging London. Its basic conclusions were persuasive even if too much attention was paid to Carnaby Street. For instance: 'Britain has lost an empire and lightened the pound. In the process, it has also recovered a lightness of heart lost during the weighty centuries of world leadership. Much of the world still thinks of Britain as the land of Victorianism, but Victorianism was only a temporary aberration in the British character, which is basically less inhibited than most. London today is in many ways like a cheerful, violent, lusty town of William Shakespeare . . .'

* André Deutsch, London, 1978

Then again: 'Today, Britain is in the midst of a bloodless revolution. This time, those who are giving way are the old Tory-Liberal Establishment that ruled the Empire from the clubs along Pall Mall and St. James's, the still powerful financial City of London, the Church and Oxbridge. In their stead is rising a new and surprising leadership . . . Says sociologist Richard Hoggart, 47, himself a slum orphan from industrial Leeds: "A new group of people is emerging into society, creating a kind of classlessness and a verve which has not been seen before."'

It was possible to believe in 1966 that *Time* as well as Hoggart had got it right. What went wrong? Another American, Senator Daniel P. Moynihan of New York, provided a somewhat jaundiced view in his book, *A Dangerous Place**. Moynihan, a gregarious Irish-American who was a post-graduate at the London School of Economics before launching into his colourful career as an academic, diplomat and politician, placed the blame squarely on what he saw as the British Revolution, the fourth revolution to influence the course of history in the last two hundred years.

The first two took place in America and France in the late eighteenth century, and emphasized constitutional rights and individual liberties. The antithesis, the Russian Revolution, created the totalitarian state. Then came the British Revolution, whose welfare state was seen to be a synthesis of the American and Russian revolutions. 'The first fact about British socialism was that it contained a suspicion of, almost a bias against, economic development. It had emerged in the age of the Diamond Jubilee, and was fixed in its belief that there was plenty of wealth to go around if only it were fairly distributed. Redistribution, not production, remained central to the ethos of British socialism. Profit became synonymous with exploitation. With one or another variant this attitude was to be found throughout the former British world (with further variants in former European colonies). Contrary argument had but little effect, nor did experience, as witness the performance of the British economy itself in "the collective age"'.

The early British socialists were not wholly to blame. Those with upper-middle or middle-class backgrounds shared many attitudes and assumptions with contemporaries who belonged to the Conservative party. Tories also believed that there was sufficient wealth; not to be fairly distributed of course, but to be administered rather than developed. Britain had become an administrative nation long before the rise of middle-class socialism, or limousine liberalism as it is known in the United States. That was the first role it chose for itself after the period of

* Little, Brown. Boston. 1978

3

imperial expansion, the second being a world power to defend the empire.

That is why the best brains went into the Indian Civil Service and the Foreign Office, lesser brains into the armed forces, the Colonial Service and colonial police, and the also-rans into tea and rubber plantations and trading houses in entrepot ports such as Singapore. That is why, despite bad consciences and self-promoting propaganda, the empire was not ruthlessly exploited commercially. Indeed, the ICS believed its sacred duty was to defend Indians against the boxwallahs, as businessmen were derisively dismissed. With this brain drain and diversion of attention at the top, the British home economy inevitably fell behind that of the United States and Germany, and eventually Japan and most other industrial democracies. This historical process brought about gentrification; that is the sons of successful manufacturers and iron masters joined the gentry instead of expanding the family wealth. Education was a vital step towards social respectability, and Professor Hugh Thomas blamed public schools because of their emphasis on classical education. Latin studies, he argued, conditioned young minds for public service, and the empire provided the opportunity.

Economic development, like the money it generates, does not necessarily bring happiness, but Nossiter's conclusions about our condition in the last quarter of the twentieth century were too comforting and misleading. I do not believe that instead of being the sick man of Europe Britain is once again leading the world into a civilized post-industrial age. I would be happy, given the right to work as hard as I want to work, to live in a society where men and women can cultivate their gardens; and leisure, books, music and the arts generally are valued as much as a new car or coloured television set. That, alas, is not the Britain I live in, and I do not believe that as a nation we have made a conscious choice.

The evidence is to the contrary. We are not a society at peace with ourselves. Most of us are no longer proud of being British. Class tensions in the Marxist sense have largely replaced the old class system. In the early seventies the then Tory Prime Minister, Edward Heath, spoke of the unacceptable face of capitalism, and the trade unions have since revealed an equally unacceptable face. To quote Barbara Hammond, the Labour party exalted the humble and meek and redistributed the wealth, and unfortunately the humble and meek turned very nasty in the process. Some of us are not so tolerant as we once were, and collectively are less rather than more humane.

That said, I have continually met decent people who want the kind of society Nossiter wrote about. They want to do an honest day's work, do their duty by the community, cultivate their gardens or allotments, love their wives and do well by their children. I am convinced that they are the majority, but despite the expansion of democratic processes their modest ambitions and political concepts have been ignored or misrepresented. British society is in a state of disequilibrium; or in the sublime words of the general confession of the Book of Common Prayer, there is no health in us.

Why? Arguably all would now be well if we had got the economy right. Certainly it would have helped if the Treasury knights had done their sums correctly, if managers had managed efficiently and the trade unions had recognized that the best interests of their members would be better served by achieving higher productivity. So much is obvious, but our economic troubles are largely political, social and ideological in origin. Only the consequences are economic. The political parties, Parliament, the Civil Service and ourselves must share the blame.

Other factors not easily definable have also played a part. Ancient strengths tended to become weaknesses in that our romanticism, our reluctance to face facts and our general cussedness, which explained much of our history, were apparently ill-suited to the modern world. Our sense of national greatness and superiority stood between us and the new realities. We went on behaving as if we were still a great power, the centre of an empire which we were busily dissolving, because we saw ourselves as the partner of the United States, the new superpower.

The bureaucracy, especially the Diplomatic Service, must share the responsibility for this near-fatal delusion, but Prime Ministers and politicians of both parties were only too willing and eager to live in this pretend world. They did great damage to the country and its people in that their foreign and defence policies prevented Britain from beginning anew after the second world war. Sir Nicholas Henderson, a distinguished diplomat, had this to say in a valedictory dispatch to the Foreign Secretary in 1979*. 'Since Mr. Ernest Bevin made his plea a generation ago for more coal to give weight to his foreign policy our economic decline has been such as to sap the foundations of our diplomacy. Conversely, I believe that, during the same period, much of our foreign policy has been such as to contribute to that decline.'

Being a diplomat, Henderson got his two delicts in the wrong order. After more than thirty years of national decline he still assumed that diplomacy was somehow as important as the economic health of the country. Nevertheless, the interaction

* The *Economist*, June 2, 1979

between the two first set Britain on the slippery slope of decline.

*

Architecture provides many clues for the historian, and the pretend world of British post-war diplomacy had many epitaphs in stone. For instance, the completion of the British embassy's large chancery building in Washington more or less coincided with the real end of the Anglo-American special relationship it was intended to celebrate. Similarly the creation of Phoenix Park in Singapore, the headquarters of the British Commissioner-General for Southeast Asia, marked the approaching end of the eastern empire. In both instances the symbolism was striking, but no more than that of the Foreign and Commonwealth Office in London.

Built round an Italianate square approachable from Downing Street, the building is dominated internally by a grand staircase with heroic frescoes and statues. It would look better on the stage of Covent Garden opera house, except that the footlights would reveal its tattiness. Whenever I walked up those stairs, in earlier years following an elderly male messenger and more recently comfortable-looking mums in blue overalls of the kind worn in supermarkets, I was struck by the unspoken symbolism: pretence without much substance. I can think of no better description of British post-war foreign policy.

The Ambassador's Waiting Room, in which visitors are deposited until the Foreign Secretary is ready to receive them, is no less pretentious. It is dominated by a large-as-life portrait of the third Earl of Strafford, who helped to negotiate the Peace of Utrecht, 1711–13. He sits imperiously on a horse, and one can imagine him staring down King Philip of Spain until he renounced his claim to the French crown. One can also imagine how in the old days ambassadors of lesser countries waited apprehensively, despite diplomatic protocol, to be beckoned across the corridor into the presence of the Secretary of State for Foreign Affairs.

The beckoning is usually done by the private secretary, a young high flyer of the Diplomatic Service trained to suggest the desired degree of respect or insolence. When I called on Dr. David Owen while he was Foreign Secretary, he did the beckoning, or rather he drifted in amiably rather like a fellow member of a club to suggest it would be more agreeable to drink some port by the fire in the lobby instead of in the coffee room.

Owen was fortyish, slim and palely good-looking in a Celtic way. He wore a two-piece suit obviously bought off the peg, and could have been mistaken for a bright GP. He had a reputation for being opiniated and of being rough with his staff, but he also had the easy manner and buoyancy of comparative youth. His wife, Deborah, was American, and they lived with their three children in a gentrified house down by the river in London's East End. He was ambitious and had done very well in politics, but assumed that after his early successes bad luck would strike one day. He claimed that he would not weep if he lost his seat, a marginal, which he did in fact retain in the 1979 general election.

Owen accepted my basic proposition without any leading questions from me. It was ridiculous, he said, that such a high degree of defence expenditure and foreign representation had been maintained for so long. The 1979 level of defence spending was still too high, even in Europe where we had obvious interests to defend. He was not so sure that we could have divested ourselves of imperial and world power pretensions much quicker than we did because of deep-seated attitudes. The war had been partly to blame. We had held history at bay from Dunkirk onwards, and given that 'input of greatness' it must have been hard to make adjustments. Adjustments were always painful, and no man or political party could make a nation do what it did not want to do.

One could well ask, he continued, what would have happened to the world in those early post-war years if we had not accepted those commitments. We had first stuck to the Americans because we were determined to lock them into Europe. We could be proud of that achievement, but then the special relationship became the linchpin of British foreign policy. We could not accept our loss of power, even after Suez. We were not prepared to face reality, and many MPs still wanted to maintain forces east of Suez.

Europe offered an alternative policy, a new role, but we did not join the EEC at the beginning because we could not see ourselves as a group of offshore islands. Even Macmillan could not take his party into Europe. That was understandable if regrettable, but we refused to admit to ourselves the appalling distortion of the British economy during the war. We still dreamed of greatness while ignoring the only foundation for greatness. That was the beginning of the slide. Down the drain, if you like, he added.

Owen got up and stood by one of the many windows overlooking Horse Guards to the Admiralty beyond. From its cupolas were still slung the old aerials which had transmitted commands to the navy when Britain was great. In those far off days the Foreign Secretary was supported by a small staff and rarely delegated authority. Owen was assisted by four Ministers of State, three parliamentary under-secretaries and a host of senior officials.

Rather morosely, Owen said that while Britain pretended to be a great power the country allowed itself to be boxed in by the bureaucracy and to be ruled by committee. The Labour party had also equated socialism with centralism. The Tories were just as bad, and their reorganization of local government in the early seventies was one of the great tragedies of the century. They had screwed it up, as their reorganization had screwed up the National Health Service. Both parties believed too much in administrative solutions, which was why new governments invariably reorganize the departments. Quangos (quasi-autonomous non-governmental organizations) were a bloody disgrace.

Celtic fire suddenly blazed in his eyes. 'We have got to get off our ass', he said. That Americanism was rarely heard in Britain, which perhaps helped to explain the malaise. We had to take risks, Owen added, and be more daring. We must recover our dynamism, recapture our self-confidence and revive the spirit of the old merchant adventurers.

*

We spoke a kind of shorthand used by politicians and journalists when discussing a subject both know well, and as Owen looked out to the Admiralty building, the memory of Ernest Bevin, the first post-war Foreign Secretary, emerged from the back of my mind.

I first met him in the thirties in London's East End. I was very young, and was both attracted and rather frightened by a crowd of angry dockers outside the old Stepney Town Hall in Cable Street. They had called an unofficial strike and Bevin, who then ran the Transport and General Workers' Union, was haranguing them from the steps. His face was heavy behind the spectacles, and he exuded an authority I have never forgotten. He said, almost snarlingly, that they would strike when he told them to strike and not before. His declamation was spiced with four-letter words. He dominated the erstwhile angry crowd, and eventually they yielded and drifted away. A few gave him a cheer as he stomped off – even in those early days he had bad feet – in the direction of Shadwell Underground station. I realized that he had won when the dockers, all of them casual labourers, lined up outside our mother's coffee shop next morning for work.

Ernie Bevin, as he was widely known, was a born leader. He first went to work at the age of thirteen for sixpence a week and his keep, and by sheer force of personality rose through the ranks of the trade union movement to become the boss of the Transport and General Workers' Union and President of the Trades Union

Congress. Churchill appointed him Minister of Labour and National Service during the second world war, and he became Foreign Secretary in the post-war Labour government.

It was a critical juncture in British history. The war had destroyed the old balance of world power. Britain, although victorious and nominally co-equal with the United States and the Soviet Union, was exhausted. Her economic assets had been ruthlessly spent in support of the war effort. Her people were tired, and the 1945 general election proved beyond doubt that they rejected the imperial world power ambitions of Churchill. The Labour government was committed to the independence of India, and eventually of all the colonial dependencies. This unprecedented act of self-abnegation, together with economic exhaustion, was bound to reduce Britain to a group of mist-shrouded off-shore islands of little more importance than they were before adventurers such as Sir Francis Drake, Captain John Smith and Captain James Cook started it all by sailing away to claim much of the earth for Britain.

In retrospect there was every reason to accept the inevitable. Britain had made its mark on history. Its empire was larger than Rome, and arguably its achievements greater and more lasting. The time had come to begin again, not by docilely accepting the new straitened circumstances but by looking for new worlds to conquer in trade, technology and, above all, in the development of the British people. We were a talented people. The war had demonstrated that we were courageous, adventurous and resourceful. Its successful prosecution had given the nation's leaders great self-confidence. There were huge reserves of good will to be tapped in the old Commonwealth until we got to our feet again. The newly-established United Nations, then largely under Anglo-American control, could have been a suitable agency for the disposal of the colonies. We could have started afresh, and with every chance of success.

It was not to be. Soviet imperialism could not be ignored or left entirely to the Americans to contain. Having defeated and devastated Germany, British troops could not be pulled out before an acceptable successor government was established. We had obvious interests and responsibilities in Europe, but there was no rational reason for Britain to continue to shoulder the responsibilities of a world power. Australia and New Zealand were seeking the American protection already enjoyed by Canada. With the passing of empire, we could have honourably accepted the diminished role of a medium-sized trading nation. Certainly there was no reason why Bevin, who had fought for working men and women most of his life, should cling to a world role.

It was a measure of the times and the ethos of the country that a man such as Bevin responded to his new job as if he was an Old Etonian who had served in the Brigade of Guards and lunched regularly at the Carlton Club. He was not alone. Emanuel Shinwell was afterwards remembered fondly by the generals and admirals as the best Minister of Defence they had served under. The British people were condemned to continuing deprivation and, worse, denied the opportunity of creating a new Britain because men such as Bevin and Shinwell, despite their working-class background and politics, preferred not to recognize that the days of imperial greatness were over. They refused to be consuls at sunset.

Not that Bevin was unaware of Britain's weaknesses. Clement Attlee, the Prime Minister, privately regarded him as the bedrock of the Cabinet because of his strength and sense of realism. In the immediate post-war years American intentions were not wholly clear and until 1948 Bevin could not be certain that Washington would accept the responsibilities of super power. He also believed that the Anglo-American joint-production committees and the Marshall Plan would renew and strengthen the economy, that once again Britain would be great; but the most persuasive factor was the national habit of authority. Britain had been the centre of a vast empire too long willingly to accept the inevitable. That applied alike to working-class socialists and aristocratic Tories.

The war, truly a world war unlike the 1914–18 war, had also extended the country's world role. Even after demobilization the budgets and operations of the armed services and the Foreign Office were much larger and more extensive than in 1939. With forces stationed from the Elbe river to the Pacific, few political leaders and senior civil servants questioned the assumption that Britain had the means as well as the responsibility for helping to shape the future of the world.

This habit of authority, buttressed by national and personal pride, prevented Britain from getting rid of the burden of the past, and was the main reason why Britain failed to seek a new role and take full advantage of the post-war boom. Apart from the almost insupportable demands it made upon the country's human and other resources, this illusion of world power distracted attention from more vital tasks. Bright young men still chose careers in the Foreign Office instead of industry. Scientists and engineers were too busy making the Bomb and other sophisticated weapons to contribute much to the modernization of industry. That was left to the Americans, and afterwards to the West Germans and Japanese. The press, including *The Times*, was no less captive of the imperial past.

Obeisances were ritually made towards the uncertain future and the great opportunities awaiting us. The Festival of Britain was an obvious example, but the national agenda remained unchanged. Opinion-makers as well as politicians and officials still applied their minds to the problems of defence and diplomacy despite the introduction of the welfare state and the rising expectations of ordinary people. They were doubly blind. For instance, in the western zones of occupied Germany the British helped to create a trades union movement worthy of a modern industrial democracy, but failed to realize that their own unions needed to be dragged into the modern world.

The historic opportunity for genuine reform was thus missed. No wonder Dean Acheson twenty years later observed that Britain has lost an empire and had failed to find a new role. That observation of the former Secretary of State was bitterly resented at the time. I can remember the embassy in Washington waspishly saying, off the record of course, that Acheson spoke only for himself. Their resentment, and that of their lords and masters in London, was all the more bitter because the Anglo-American special relationship was supposed to have given Britain a new role. Given that pretence, they could not accept the truth although Acheson was a friend of Britain and had worked closely with Bevin.

The claims for the special relationship were many and varied, but originally it was in fact the product of national self-interests, mutually but only briefly compatible. Confined almost exclusively to defence and diplomacy, it should have died a natural death in the early post-war years. It remained a pillar of British foreign policy because it helped to maintain the illusion of power. Harold Macmillan even had the impertinence to claim that Britain was the Greece to the new American Rome.

Perhaps the special relationship with the United States was a psychologically necessary stage in the retreat from empire and world power although American interests generally prevailed whenever the policies of the two countries differed. The most dramatic was the 1956 Suez crisis, but American generosity was on the whole more damaging than the alleged selfishness. One obvious example was the frequent rescue operations mounted to save the pound, which permitted Britain to stumble from crisis to crisis without trying to put her house in order. Another was President Kennedy's decision to provide the Royal Navy with Polaris missiles against the advice of officials such as George Ball.

The gesture went against the general trend of American nuclear policy at the time. It maintained Britain's illusions of power and

11

delayed her entry into Europe. Quite early in his Administration, Kennedy had intimated to Harold Macmillan that Britain's place was not somewhere in mid-Atlantic but in the European Economic Community. Alas, even that wise old politician would not listen. The missile deal was negotiated at Nassau in the Bahamas, and an offended President de Gaulle blackballed Britain's application to join the Community.

It was the second time Britain had missed the European boat, but the first was perhaps understandable. Centuries of national experience argued against throwing in our lot with continental Europe. It was something most Englishmen, myself included, felt in their bones. We were an island people. The world had been our oyster for hundreds of years. We had sailed the seven seas, planted colonies in the Americas, Australasia and Africa and in so doing had created the English-speaking world. If the wogs did not begin at Calais, Europe was filled with squabbling Frogs, Huns and Dagoes unable to govern themselves peacefully. We had saved them from themselves twice in this century, and from Napoleon in the last.

Great importance was also attached to the Commonwealth. The old Dominions, especially Australia, Canada and New Zealand, were our kith and kin. London still chose to see itself as the centre of a worldwide Commonwealth whose bounds, to paraphrase *Land of Hope and Glory*, would be set wider still and wider as the former colonies graduated to full membership. Sheer romanticism of course, but the Commonwealth was seen to reinforce the Anglo-American special relationship. The unspoken assumption was that it would make the relationship less unequal.

The British are a romantic people, I often think of them as the Latin Americans of northern Europe; but it is now difficult to accept that grown men could have believed such nonsense. One ignored reality was the essential weakness of the Commonwealth. Apart from Australian, Canadian and New Zealand dependence upon the United States for their national security, Pandit Nehru, the Prime Minister of India, was disdainful of Americans; he shared the contempt of most of his fellow Old Harrovians and was working actively to create a non-aligned bloc more suspicious of the United States than of the Soviet Union. South Africa was an embarrassment until it quit, and India and Pakistan fought each other at frequent intervals. The new African members seemed to regard the acceptance of the Commonwealth as a painless and meaningless price to pay for independence. Regular conferences of Commonwealth Prime Ministers papered over the cracks, but only temporarily. The pious hope that somehow the Commonwealth would be a bridge between the white, yellow, brown and black races survived in Whitehall but in few other capitals.

The romantics also ignored the fact that Britain was already in Europe. As a member of Nato she was committed to maintaining armed forces on the European continent. Those bright Oxbridge chaps in Whitehall were prepared to shoulder that burden, which became more onerous with each passing year, while denying themselves the economic opportunities of EEC membership. By the late fifties the opportunities could no longer be ignored; Britain took the plunge but the price of the internal contradictions of a British policy built on self-delusion was de Gaulle's blackball.

*

The Permanent Under-Secretary for Foreign and Commonwealth Affairs, Sir Michael Palliser KCMG, personified the Diplomatic Service of which he was also head. The son of an admiral, the product of Wellington College and Merton, Oxford, he fought with the Coldstream Guards during the war and entered the Diplomatic Service in 1947. He served in Athens, Brussels, Dakar and Paris, and his last post before returning to London was Ambassador and Permanent Representative to the European Communities. His wife was the daughter of the late Paul-Henri Spaak, the Belgian and European statesman, and he was a Chevalier of the Order of Orange Nassau and of the Légion d'Honneur. Almost inevitably, his club was Buck's.

This is a portrait of an elitist, and he looked every inch the part. The palely-handsome face was disciplined, and the blue eyes were unlikely to betray emotion involuntarily. He spoke easily and with great assurance. The sentences emerged complete, without hesitation or infelicity. His well-stocked mind was clearly equal to any situation. One could understand why he was selected to be private secretary first to the Foreign Secretary and then the Prime Minister, the highest perches for Whitehall high flyers before they are rewarded with posts of power and influence.

And yet he failed the diplomatic entrance examination the first time he sat, and some of his basic attitudes were hardly elitist. For instance, he believed that one reason for Britain's decline was the educational system, and if he could have his time over again would prefer to attend a state school. His own children attended French state schools. His wife went through the Belgian state system, and, I must add that nobody could dismiss Lady Palliser as uneducated and uncivilized. She could look formidable on official occasions, but because of those years of egalitarian education had none of the side of some British ambassadors' wives.

Palliser worked in a grand office no smaller than that of the Foreign Secretary, but his feet were firmly on the ground. He appeared to be more aware of Britain's lost opportunities than of the trappings of office. He was a convinced Europeanist, believing that a diminished Britain could best prosper as a loyal member of the European Community, and he was converted long before his political masters. He was working on the German desk in the old FO when the European Coal and Steel Community was being negotiated in 1950, and recalled reading the reports of the British observer with despair.

Not that he apportioned blame. The first post-war Labour government, he conceded, not unnaturally regarded the founders of the European Community as a clique of right-wing Roman Catholics. Some Labour politicians were anxious not to shut out eastern Europe, a view shared at the time by the West German Social Democrats. The Tories thought that they were a cut above continental Europeans, which was again understandable if regrettable, because France, Germany and Italy were in a bit of a mess at the time. The Tories changed their minds as the Community developed, but their proposed free trade area was essentially a spoiling action. Harold Wilson still hankered after a world role when Labour returned to power in 1964, but two years later recognized that Britain's future was in Europe.

Palliser did not know this when he was invited to become one of Wilson's private secretaries, and for that reason did not accept immediately. He had his European idealism as well as ambition, and said as much when he walked across to No 10 to see Wilson. He was honoured, he said, but perhaps because of his attachment to the European idea, the Prime Minister should look for another man. Only then did Wilson indicate that he had changed his mind, and was planning to seek membership.

Like other high flyers who served Wilson at No 10 in the early years, Palliser had a great respect for him. He said that Wilson was astute, quick thinking and not, as was generally supposed, only a clever politician quick on his feet. He was a good strategist, who could look into the future and plan accordingly but was an atrocious tactician. His mistakes were mainly tactical, and they eventually brought about his downfall.

Palliser helped Edward Heath to negotiate entry into Europe, but Britain had again missed the boat – the post-war tide of economic development as well as the opportunities to shape the Community in its own image. The growing worldwide recession and the oil crisis of 1973 were double blows. Everybody suffered, but Britain more so because of her industrial weakness. What was to have been an irrevocable commitment became unstuck. Britain's future was once again in doubt. Atavistic suspicions of Europe were revived, and some politicians still thought that they had to choose between Europe and the United States, but it was no longer a matter of choice. We needed friends, Palliser said, and they were in the Community. We had only to cooperate, and we could make a go of it.

*

Palliser was not typical of his generation in the Foreign Office. Too many of them had been reluctant to abandon the pretensions of world power. Self-delusion was fostered by the grandeur of some of the embassies in which they served; Paris, Rome and Washington are obvious examples. Ambassadors also represent the Monarch and not the Prime Minister. The Queen has no power, of course, but one fiction encouraged another. During my years as a foreign correspondent, I met more than one British ambassador who behaved as if Britain still ruled the waves, and as if in some metaphysical way he represented a power grander than the incumbent government. They are now a dying breed. The new men are more realistic if only because they have grown up in the shadow of American and Soviet super power. Most of them are intelligent, perhaps too intelligent because the Diplomatic Service still attracts brains which could be more usefully employed elsewhere. It is still too large despite two attempts to reduce its functions.

The Review Committee on Overseas Expenditure investigated the Foreign Service in the late sixties and its report said that Britain was no longer a great power and should act accordingly. 'If Britain may be compared to a man who decided that his requirements no longer justify the upkeep of a Rolls-Royce, the choice lies between replacing it by a smaller car of high quality or a lower quality car of the same size.' The committee preferred the former and recommended cuts up to ten percent.

Its report achieved little. Ambassadors continued to ride in Rolls-Royce cars and act as if they represented a great power. British diplomats remained more numerous than their West German and Japanese colleagues, and entertained more lavishly. A grandiose embassy designed by Basil Spence and fit for an oil sheikh was built in Rome. The British Ambassador to the Organization for Economic Cooperation and Development was given a Paris flat costing £380,000 when the pound was still worth, say, fifteen bob. The ambassador to Brazil, stationed in the new capital of Brasilia and no doubt resenting its rawness, was given a

15

flat in Rio de Janeiro which cost £191,000. Rio is an infinitely more attractive city than Brasilia, but that is hardly a reason for providing the ambassador with such an expensive weekend pad at the taxpayers' expense.

The Central Policy Review Staff under its director, Sir Kenneth Berrill, took another look at overseas representation nearly ten years later. The Berrill Report proved to be a very blunt instrument. The so-called think tank did not seem fully to understand the intricacies of diplomacy, but rightly suggested that political and diplomatic attitudes had not kept up with the reality of Britain's declining power. It recommended closure of twenty embassies and thirty-five consulates, the abolition of the British Council, the merger of the Diplomatic Service with the Home Civil Service and the creation of a Foreign Service Group to concentrate on the promotion of exports.

The recommendations were largely rejected of course. Staff levels were reduced, but Owen bitterly said that while elderly messengers and clerks were declared redundant the senior staff at the FCO was actually increased. Palliser said that his service was still burdened with expensive ornaments of our imperial past. The chancery building in Washington was much too large, and he dreamed of having it torn down and moving the staff back into the old Lutyens building. He also dreamed of selling the new embassy in Rome and replacing it with two rented floors of a modest office building.

The opportunity came in 1979 when the Thatcher government demanded spending cuts in all government departments. Alas, the Rome embassy was not sold to the King of Saudi Arabia, and that weekend pad in Rio did not go to the highest bidder. Instead, the FCO tried to cut the External Services of the BBC although Bush House projected Britain more effectively and cheaply than the combined efforts of British embassies and consulates around the world. No matter that the services were the envy of the United States and the Soviet Union. When it came to the crunch the FCO preferred the pretend world of grand embassies.

A backbench revolt in Parliament prevented too much damage being done to the External Services, but the imperial past still bewitched the politicians. The approaching end of the operational life of the Polaris submarine fleet gave the country the opportunity to dismantle its nuclear force, its last ridiculous claim to being a great power. With the boats sent to the breaker's yard we could have finally adjusted ourselves to our diminished status. Instead, in 1979 the Tory government planned to replace them with Trident submarines at an estimated cost of £6,000 million. We were committed to remaining a nuclear power until the second decade of the twenty-first century when, if the national decline continued, Britain would have been relegated from the second to the third or fourth division of economic and military powers.

That prospect made a third generation of nuclear weapons doubly absurd, but not for the leaders of the two major political parties. Mrs. Margaret Thatcher went to Washington to negotiate the Trident order, but before the defeat of the Labour government, a small and secret Cabinet committee under the chairmanship of the Prime Minister, James Callaghan, had been unwilling to accept unilateral nuclear disarmament. Denis Healey, who as Chancellor knew that Britain could ill afford it, had gone along with the Prime Minister despite the advice of his own civil servants. Later the Treasury knights were to use forceful language rarely seen in official minutes in a final attempt to drag the Tories back to reality, but even they, the most powerful official group in Whitehall, were defeated.

It was difficult to understand why. The politicians and the admirals, generals and air marshals must have known that our national security depended upon the American nuclear umbrella, and in the unlikely event of that being withheld, there was little or nothing we could do to prevent eventual subjugation by the Soviet Union. The only conclusion to be drawn was that more than twenty years after Suez little or nothing had been learned. They were still hankering after the past and ignoring the reality of the present.

TWO

Who Rules?

The defeat of the Tory government in 1974 was a traumatic event for Britain; not the departure of the Prime Minister, Edward Heath, but the manner of his going. The miners' strike with its secondary picketing led to headlines asking who ruled Britain, but the answer was certainly not the miners or the trade union movement generally. They could bring the country to its knees, but not rule. They could wage industrial guerrilla warfare as destructive as urban terrorism, but the union leaders could not even control their shock troops. The question was whether Britain was still governable, or to put it another way, whether our constitutional system was adequate for the challenges of our times. To answer that question I first had to remind myself of the strengths and weaknesses of our unwritten Constitution.

The official handbook *Britain** says that the supreme legislative authority in the United Kingdom is the Queen in Parliament, that is to say, the Queen and the two Houses of Parliament – the House of Lords and the elected House of Commons. Parliament is not subject to the type of legal restraints imposed on legislatures with formal written constitutions. It is virtually free to legislate as it pleases: generally to make or unmake any law; to legalize past illegalities and make void and punishable what was lawful when done and thus reverse the decisions of the ordinary courts; and to destroy established conventions or turn a convention into binding law. It can prolong its own life beyond the normal period without consulting the electorate.

In practice, the handbook continues, Parliament is slow to exercise its supremacy in this way. Its Members bear in mind the Common Law which has grown up in Britain throughout the centuries and act as far as possible in accordance with precedent and tradition. Moreover, although the validity of an Act of Parliament cannot be disputed in the law courts, no Parliament would be likely to pass an Act which it knew would receive no public support. The system of party government ensures that Parliament legislates with its responsibility to the electorate in mind.

* HMSO, London, 1979

The behaviour of Members on the floor of the House is indeed dictated by precedent and tradition, but otherwise this official version is no longer wholly true. Even if it was, the inherent instability of a system based on the supremacy of Parliament should be obvious to those not blinded by the grandeur of British constitutional history. Apart from the archaic politenesses, the Mother of Parliaments is not always a shrewd and benign matron conscious of the past and mindful of her responsibilities to the electorate and future generations. The government of the day can be oblivious of the past, resentful of convention and conscious only of its own power. It can and does ride roughshod over the Opposition and minority interests and opinion. Without constitutional safeguards such as the separation of powers and the checks and balances of the American system, Parliament is in a very real sense above the law. I am convinced that this is a major reason for Britain's decline.

The inherent instability will be explored later, but supremacy is at least in part responsible for the dangerous degree of overcentralization which helps to make efficient government increasingly difficult. Parliament is now expected to resolve all the country's problems. No longer believing in God, we seem to believe that Parliament is the supreme being; that it is capable of declaring original sin null and void. This heresy has its attractions for many Members; for those who want to turn back the clock, or create a socialist state, or believe that they can reverse the country's decline by strong leadership.

Edward Heath was such a man. Robust and authoritative, he looked every inch a born leader. As a former smallboat sailor I would have been happy to have him at the helm in a Force 10 gale, even though he could shake like a jelly on the plate when laughing. He was supposed to have been typical of the post-war meritocracy, the men and women who began on the bottom rungs of the ladder and quickly ascended to the top. His rapid rise to political power increased his self-confidence. He had great vision and drive, and eventually succeeded in taking Britain into Europe, but he was not a natural politician. I think that *Private Eye* got him about right in its Heathco series. He was born to be the chairman of a large corporation or Chief of the Defence Staff and not the Prime Minister of a country which can only be ruled with the assent of the governed.

Vic Feather, the late general secretary of the Trades Union Congress, once told me with wry humour of what happened when he was invited to No 10 to discuss incomes policy. He assumed that discussion meant negotiation and compromise, but found that he was expected to take orders with a touch of the forelock as if he was a foreman of a Victorian mill. With that in mind, I asked Heath soon after his defeat in 1974 what lessons he had learned which would be helpful when he returned to Downing Street. I was careful to say when and not if, but he glared at me and devoted the remainder of the lunch hour to explain, evidently to his own satisfaction, that everybody was out of step except him. A slight case of megalomania common to most leaders perhaps, but surely enhanced by the supremacy of Parliament.

Heath was also the victim of over-centralization. He was expected to do too much and tried too hard. As Douglas Hurd, his political secretary at the time, suggested in his own account of the last dreadful months of his Administration,* Heath and his Cabinet colleagues at first thrived on the excitement and did not notice the onset of fatigue. Then, because he allowed himself no respite, his pace slackened and he began to miss his stroke. In the end, and this is my conclusion, he was not fit to govern.

One should not sneer. It was to happen to other Ministers psychologically better equipped than Heath for the give and take of politics. Even the working lives of ordinary Ministers can be onerous enough in times of domestic peace and plenty. They have to run their departments, take their turn at the dispatch box at Question Time, and lead off or conclude debates which can continue far into the night. They must attend Cabinet meetings where they have to fight for their departments, and after inevitable compromise and trimming must account for themselves to the party and their constituents.

The Heath government enjoyed neither domestic peace nor plenty, and they took office in a combative mood. They were determined to rescue the country from the assumed snares, delusions and inefficiencies of Wilsonian socialism. Entry into Europe and the Industrial Relations Act of 1971, to mention only two items on their agenda, would have been enough for any government, but the economy went wrong again and an incomes policy was introduced. They were in full retreat, and events were crowding in by early October 1973. Phase three of the incomes policy was made all the more difficult by dissension within the Cabinet, and Arab oil sanctions and the miners' determination to break pay restraint threatened economic disaster as well as another shaming political defeat. A state of emergency was declared and the three-day week imposed.

The government was in disarray when the new year dawned, and Heath and his colleagues began to think about going to the country. His mind was made up when the miners voted overwhelmingly to strike again. On February 5, after dinner at

* *An End to Promises*, Collins, London 1979

Pruniers, Heath explained his desperate worry about what was at stake. Everything he had tried to do was at risk. No one pressed him that evening. Events had already overwhelmed Heath and his Cabinet.

James Callaghan and his Cabinet were similarly overwhelmed five years later when the unions baulked at phase four of yet another incomes policy. He had accepted the arithmetic of his anti-inflation policy, and tried to hold wage rises down to five per cent. There was no reason why they should have been more; the inflation rate was coming down and living standards were rising slowly although productivity had remained static. Public opinion polls indicated that a majority of the work force was willing to give it a go. In a better-organized society the policy would have been pursued further, but in Britain it was political madness.

To some extent Callaghan was better prepared than Heath for the crisis that followed because he had long anticipated it. At the 1978 Labour party conference in Blackpool he had taken me aside in his avuncular way, and said, 'Lou, we are in for a long, bleak winter.' The inference was that if the unions in effect declared civil war the damage done to the social fabric and economy would make them finally realize that restraint and common sense were essential if they and the country were to survive. It was a painful and possibly effective remedy, but the concordat which emerged after talks with the unions did not offer much hope for the future. It seemed that nothing had been learned, and he and his Cabinet colleagues were no less exhausted than Heath five years earlier. For instance, Callaghan misjudged the mood of the electorate when after returning from a summit conference in the Caribbean he blandly denied that the country was in crisis. Some days the responses of Ministers such as Merlyn Rees and David Ennals at Question Time hardly made sense. They were at the end of their tether.

Rees had been one of the Cabinet's walking wounded since leaving the Northern Ireland Office. He had been over-worked, and was still a prime target for IRA gunmen. The strain must have been intolerable, as I discovered when we dined at the home of the American Minister in London. He was relaxed and chatting amiably when we left together, but at the door suggested I should stand aside. It was opened by a servant, and suddenly he was silhouetted against the glare of many lights. The quiet Kensington street seemed filled with police cars, and armed Special Branch men waited to shepherd him to his car. He gave me a half-apologetic smile and walked unhurriedly down the steps.

He was transferred to the Home Office, where life was supposed to be a little easier, but towards the end of his term one of his

21

senior civil servants told me that he had still not recovered from his Ulster experience. On more than one occasion when they were discussing some problem, say in Birmingham or Manchester, he would unwittingly refer to the city as Belfast.

Rees was a very decent and brave man, although not as tough as Denis Healey who served as Defence Minister for six years and Chancellor of the Exchequer for five. Both jobs were very demanding. He was responsible for finally bringing the troops back from the old imperial glacis east of Suez, and the launching of the Polaris submarine fleet. He had introduced cost-benefit analysis and other American managerial techniques to the Ministry of Defence, and at Nato had created the nuclear defence affairs committee and nuclear planning group as alternatives to giving nuclear weapons to West Germany. At the Treasury, where he was responsible for fourteen budgets, he had doggedly settled down to the long-term policy of curbing inflation.

Healey was often attacked by the extreme Left of his own party, first by foolish men who believed that the defence of the kingdom could be left to the tender loving care of the Soviet Union and then by those who believed that the economy would best flourish under siege conditions. He had to contend with the 1975 wages explosion, which led to another round of wage restraint. He negotiated the loan from the International Monetary Fund and reduced the public sector borrowing requirement.

Healey survived because of his unusual physical and intellectual toughness. He was once called an intellectual thug, and his red face with its blue eyes twinkling under bushy brows exuded rude health, but towards the end of the Callaghan Administration he confessed to envying his American and European colleagues. They led fairly normal lives and had time to think because their governmental systems were not nearly as demanding as Westminster. There would have to be reforms eventually, he preferred some form of devolution; but meanwhile the system would continue to exhaust lesser men.

Good government cannot be expected from exhausted men, and Ministers are not the only victims of the system. The Commons sits many more hours a year than other Parliaments, on an average at least twice as many as the United States Congress and five times as many as the West German Bundestag.

*

We could once take pride in Parliament. We, the British, invented modern political democracy, and had ruled ourselves, at least some of us did, when the rest of Europe was still misruled by absolute monarchs. We displayed considerable political genius over the centuries, a genius which when exported to North America, Australia and New Zealand created other effective systems of government. The old Westminster system had its faults; even between the Reform Acts and the second world war, Parliament was largely run by and for the benefit of the middle classes and business and landed interests. It was not always effective by the simple standards of the time, but HH the Pope himself is supposed to be infallible only in faith and morals. Then something went wrong in the fifties and early sixties. The subsequent state of the country was proof of that, and those who argued with some cause that the government should not be held wholly responsible could not ignore the parlous condition of Parliament.

To find out what went wrong we must ignore the official version of how the Constitution works, and look back to the periods when Parliament did function reasonably well. Alexis de Tocqueville, the author of *Democracy in America*, provides a good beginning. His report on England and Ireland appeared in *Oeuvres Complètes*, which was edited by J. P. Mayer and published under the title *Journeys to England and Ireland*. Mayer wrote, 'I know of no more penetrating book written on the British political mind. Tocqueville was indeed the Montesquieu of the nineteenth century and his interpretations reach far into the future which has become our present.'

Tocqueville's present was the Britain of the first Reform Bill, and the aristocracy was still in control. Nearly everything was run for their benefit, including the universities. At Oxford he was surprised to find that education was not free despite the wealth of the university. He listened to the Duke of Wellington in the House of Lords, and was not impressed. 'It was the strangest sight to see the man, who had won so many battles and defeated Bonaparte, as embarrassed as a child reciting its lesson before a pitiless pedagogue.'

But he was impressed by the survival of the aristocracy, and was among the first to see that flexibility was its strength. Unlike the old French nobility, it was open to recruits from below. It accepted the newly rich of the industrial revolution, and being thus continually enriched and renewed, continued to have a hand in everything. He was no less impressed by British class consciousness. 'The French wish not to have superiors. The English wish to have inferiors. The Frenchman constantly raises his eyes above him with anxiety. The Englishman lowers his beneath him with satisfaction.'

Tocqueville was born an aristocrat but accepted democracy as inevitable. He was, however, apprehensive because he was half persuaded that democracy and its attendant centralization were not compatible with personal liberty. He believed that centralization was a democratic instinct, and would lead to despotism. Nevertheless, he had high hopes for liberty in Britain where the growth of centralization was obstructed by 'laws, habits, manners, the English rebellious spirit against general or unfirm ideas, but fond of peculiarities . . .

'In England the centralization of government is carried to great perfection; the state has the vigour of one man, and its will puts immense masses in motion and turns its whole power where it pleases. But England, which has done such great things for the last fifty years, has never centralized its administration. Indeed, I cannot conceive that a nation can live and prosper without a powerful centralization of government. But I am of the opinion that a centralized administration is fit only to enervate the nation in which it exists, by incessantly diminishing their local spirit.'

The energies released by the industrial revolution, and the urge to make money, reminded Tocqueville of the United States. After visiting Birmingham, he said, 'They work as if they must get rich by the evening and die the next day. They are generally very intelligent people, but intelligent in the American way.' He saw great virtue in their industry, and thought he saw how liberty could become compatible with democracy and equality and survive in Britain. He was persuaded of a hidden relationship between liberty and trade.

'Looking at the turn given to the human spirit in England by political life; seeing the Englishman, certain of the support of his laws, relying on himself and unaware of any obstacle except the limit of his own powers, acting without constraint; seeing him, inspired by the sense that he can do anything, looking restlessly at what now is, always in search of the best, seeing him like that, I am in no hurry to enquire whether his nature has scooped out ports for him, and given him iron and coal. The reason for his commercial prosperity is not there at all: it is in himself.'

The author of the classic *Democracy in America* had a wider and deeper concept of politics than most observers. Walter Bagehot was more concerned with the machinery of government, presumably because he was a political journalist, and in *The English Constitution* he examined its working during the classical period of parliamentary government; that is before Disraeli's Reform Bill was enacted in 1867. He was among the first to look beyond the established view of the Queen in Parliament; indeed, he argued that the appendages of monarchy had been converted into the essence of a republic.

For Bagehot, the prime function of the House of Commons was

to elect a Cabinet to rule the country, then keep an eye on its proceedings, and if necessary to dismiss it. Effective power was normally concentrated in the hands of the Prime Minister and his Cabinet. 'The efficient secret of the English Constitution may be described as the close union, the nearly complete fusion, of the executive and legislative powers.' Fusion was achieved by the Prime Minister, who exerted powers greater than those of the President of the United States. He was the managing director of a board who wielded a special control over the House of Commons because of the right of dissolution. The inner strength of the Cabinet was the combination of party loyalty, collective responsibility and secrecy.

In departmental matters Ministers were responsible to Parliament, but on all the great decisions of state the Cabinet acted collectively. Each member was free to express his views because of secrecy, but once the decision was taken they were all committed by the doctrine of collective responsibility to support it in public. Collective responsibility sharply reduced interference of the Commons in the affairs of the executive, enabled Ministers to protect their departments from 'incessant tyranny of Parliament over the public offices', and preserved for the Cabinet the initiative in legislation.

In fact, during the classical period of parliamentary government the Cabinet was not as powerful as it afterwards became. The essentials of parliamentary government were still moderation and independence of Members of Parliament. What Bagehot most liked about Parliament in his day was the existence of a solid centre; a centre composed of the majority of sensible Members collectively able to make and unmake ministries, to defy when necessary their own Whips, and above all to frustrate the growth of 'constituency government' outside. Without making government impossible, they could be a very real check on the executive.

As the late Richard Crossman noted in his preface to the Fontana edition of *The English Constitution**, in the 1860s governments suffered frequent defeats without resignation, and ministries were made and unmade without dissolution. Between 1850 and 1865 the government was defeated on an average of ten times in each session, and a majority of government supporters in many cases voted against the government. The system worked because the sense of the House usually counted more than party feeling. The Commons was the place where the most vital decisions were still taken.

The only part of these two analyses to survive in recognizable form is the power of the Cabinet; and it is interesting to note that Bagehot made the comparison between the powers of the British

* Fontana/Collins, 1963

Prime Minister and those of the American President a hundred years before modern political scientists began to complain that the man at No 10 was behaving as if he lived in the White House. All else had passed into history. Administration has been largely centralized with results that have confirmed Tocqueville's worst fears, and Members generally count for little except as voting fodder. Vital decisions are rarely made on the floor of the House because Bagehot's solid centre of sensible Members has submitted to the Whips.

Crossman also saw a flaw in Bagehot's 'efficient secret'. The change came as suffrage was extended and the modern party system developed. The right to appoint the Prime Minister, which Bagehot believed was the Commons' most important constitutional power, was gradually removed from it and shared between the parties and the Monarch. The Commons began to lose its collective will after it lost its status as an electoral college, and finally became merely the forum of debate between well-disciplined political armies. By the turn of the century the 'efficient secret' was not only the fusion of the executive and legislature in the Cabinet, but the secret links connecting the Cabinet with the party and the Civil Service.

In other words, the internal balance of Parliament changed almost beyond recognition. The individual Member was no longer responsible to his conscience and constituents, or genuinely at liberty to speak as he wished. His first responsibility was to his party because he could not expect to be re-elected without accepting its disciplines. Debates on the floor of the House could be a formality and the division that followed nearly always a foregone conclusion. It was what was said and done in the secrecy of the party meeting upstairs which was important, although the public could only hear about it through press leaks. The Opposition main party, largely denied making a contribution to debate by the disciplines of the ruling party and its own, was not so much the Loyal Opposition as a government in exile.

Crossman went on to argue that Cabinet government had been replaced by Prime Ministerial government, and not only because of his power of dissolution. This fundamental shift of power came during the second world war when Churchill imposed his personal rule on the Cabinet, Parliament and the country, and it was institutionalized by Attlee when he came to power in 1945. The significance of the shift did not become evident until the succeeding Tory government discovered that Attlee, whom Churchill once dismissed as a sheep in sheep's clothing, had decided to make Britain a nuclear power without reference to the full Cabinet. Similarly Eden afterwards ordered the Suez invasion without Cabinet consideration.

One reason for the shift was the centralization of the party machine. Another was the growth of the centralized bureaucracy; this had its own internal dynamic but the one politician who could hope to control it was the Prime Minister. The authority of the Cabinet had been further diminished by the establishment of Cabinet committees. They became necessary because of the growth of government business, the load had to be shared somehow, but as a consequence members of the Cabinet were no longer party to all the great decisions of state. Only the Prime Minister needed to know the findings of all Cabinet committees.

(The most extraordinary example of this dilution of joint Cabinet responsibility was the decision not to join the European Coal and Steel Community after the war. Neither the Foreign Secretary nor the Chancellor of the Exchequer was present when the decision was made.*)

The old doctrine of collective responsibility had nevertheless been maintained and extended downwards; from the Cabinet to junior Ministers and even private parliamentary secretaries. In other words, collective obedience was required from about one third of the government's parliamentary strength, and the Prime Minister stood at the apex of this disciplining pyramid.

Crossman's analysis was not universally accepted as gospel, if only because those politicians who worked with him were suspicious of his intellectual brilliance. Certainly his diaries, which were published later, suggested intellectual arrogance and frustration. In a *New Yorker* review, Naomi Bliven compared them with the diary of Harold Ickes, who served under Franklin Roosevelt as Secretary of the Interior. She decided that Crossman and Ickes shared a disquieting quality, the deformation of the author's character and judgement as a result of his dependence upon the Prime Minister and the President.

Shirley Williams, who was a member of the Wilson and Callaghan Cabinets, disagreed with Crossman about Prime Ministerial government. It depended upon the Prime Minister. She remembered Wilson as an accommodating, even weak chairman; Callaghan was much stronger, but he had often modified his ideas during Cabinet discussions and occasionally had reversed himself. Healey, who did not have a high opinion of Crossman, said that backbenchers could and did vote against the Whip and get away with it. The devolution debate was the obvious example.

Despite these qualifications, it is clear that Parliament does not work as it is supposed to work, and, more important, does not

* Sir Nicholas Henderson. The *Economist*, June 2, 1979

work very well. Too much power is in the hands of one person, or a small group, and without the checks and balances provided in other constitutions or by Bagehot's solid centre. The Suez fiasco might have been avoided if Eden had discussed his intentions with the full Cabinet. After all these years it is still surprising that Attlee did not seek Cabinet advice before reaching the momentous decision to make Britain a nuclear power. No less surprising, I afterwards met in Washington a British nuclear scientist who had known that the decision had been taken long before Attlee chose to take a few of his ministers into his confidence.

One does not have to be a Cabinet Minister or a political scientist to see that Parliament has also become a jousting ground where forces not necessarily representative of the national majority can impose their ideological will or whim; where legislation can be bulldozed through without proper debate; where control of the national purse strings has been largely lost because immense sums of money are voted through on the nod; and where policy can and does swing violently from the ideological left to the ideological right.

Healey thought that class attitudes must share some of the blame. He said that class differences got in the way, especially in economic debates. In West Germany, where society was relatively free of class, the Bundestag could constructively debate economic policy, but in Westminster the parties were still pushed into extreme positions because of the old class system. The Labour party had moved to the left under this compulsion while the West German Social Democrats had ceased to be Marxists. On the Tory back benches the old knights from the shires had been replaced by young businessmen whose pursuit of profits led them to prefer an older and more ruthless capitalist system.

Healey was not wholly persuasive. During the course of this enquiry the class system was held responsible for too many of the country's ills, and in this case the evidence was mixed. For instance, Tony Benn, an upper-class product of Westminster and Oxford, was on the far left of the Labour party and two Tory Prime Ministers, Edward Heath and Margaret Thatcher, were from the lower-middle class. However, there could be no doubt, whatever the reason or reasons, that British party politics had become more ideological; that some politicians, especially on the left of the Labour party, acted as if they were fighting a class war. This was very different from the old class system which appeared no longer to be much of an influence in British life except in a few areas.

Paul Rose, the Labour Member who decided to quit in 1979 after representing the Blackley constituency for fifteen years, put it more forcibly. He said that Parliament was a reflection of the ossification of institutions and attitudes responsible for Britain's decline. It did not reflect the variety and sophistication of modern society. The concept of two monolithic classes represented by the two major parties was as simplistic as applying Adam Smith's or Karl Marx's analysis of Victorian capitalism to the EEC or Comecon. The direction of the country could and did swing between these two extremes.

This of course helps to explain not only the disequilibrium in British society but also the country's disappointing economic performance. Few businesses, however efficient, can hcpe to prosper when the ground rules are changed every few years. No other modern industrial democracy has been exposed to as much violent ideological change, but then none of them has a parliament which is supreme.

*

Parliament as well as the country has become the victim of the inherent instability of its claim to supremacy. With the passing of Bagehot's solid centre, it is now defenceless against violent ideological change because supremacy does not permit the checks and balances enjoyed by other legislatures with entrenched laws. The United States Constitution, written by eighteenth-century Englishmen, is the obvious example. The founders recognized after their experiences under the British Monarch and Parliament that men and women, no matter how good and well-intentioned, could not be trusted with unlimited powers; hence the separation of powers, the checks and balances, and the Bill of Rights.

No less important than the devices to limit the power of imperfect mortals, the US Constitution recognizes that the people and not their elected representatives are supreme. This is established in the Preamble, which also defines the functions of government: 'We the People of the United States, in Order to form a more perfect Union, establish Justice, insure domestic Tranquility, provide for the common defence, promote the general Welfare, and secure the Blessings of Liberty to ourselves and our Posterity, do ordain and establish this Constitution for the United States of America.'

Strict constructionists have not always prevailed, but the essential constitutional protections have survived for nearly two hundred years. The American people are protected not only from a George the Third in republican garb but from what is known in Congress as the transient majority. For instance, unlike in Britain, their steel industry could not be nationalized, denationalized and renationalized in less than twenty years. Indeed, compulsory nationalization is unconstitutional and could not be enacted without a two-thirds majority vote to amend the Constitution. Similarly an American cannot have his or her right to work denied by expulsion from a trade union, and an American newspaper cannot be sued for publishing so-called official secrets.

Thomas Jefferson said, 'A Bill of Rights is what people are entitled to against every government on earth ... and what no just government should refuse.' The American revolutionaries believed that they were asserting the fundamental rights of Englishmen, but constitutional development in Britain was of course different. The power of the Monarch was reduced, but power was transferred to Parliament and not to the people. Parliament inherited the divine right of kings. This is the essence of parliamentary supremacy. Parliament can no more be beholden to its predecessor than one of the earlier kings could to his. The people can vote a government out of office, but cannot change Parliament. Unlike in the United States, they cannot campaign for constitutional amendments, and if they did it could be ignored by a future Parliament. The divine right of kings has now been largely inherited by the Prime Minister and Cabinet to the detriment of the Opposition and backbenchers generally. The powers of the House of Lords have been progressively reduced, and the militant members of the national executive committee of the Labour party are determined to abolish it.

There is indeed a good argument for reform, the hereditary principle is indefensible, but a strengthened second chamber is necessary if only to check the transient majority in the Commons. Nevertheless, only a simple majority would be required to make Parliament a unicameral legislature. In theory at least, the Monarch could be similarly deposed, and Britain could be declared a people's democracy or a fascist state overnight.

I am not suggesting that extremists on either wing of the political spectrum could go so far, but surely Britain must be defended against the all-powerful transient majority if it is to achieve the constitutional stability without which the national decline is unlikely to be reversed. One distinguished parliamentarian who agreed was Lord Hailsham, the former Quintin Hogg and now Lord Chancellor. Not that he wanted a written constitution, he was too English for that, but he was disturbed by what he saw as parliamentary dictatorship.

Hailsham belonged to that era of British life when politicians were admired for their parliamentary skills and philosophical understanding of politics, a background which by the sixties had persuaded many of his Tory colleagues that he was an anachronism. He also managed to look old fashioned even in his prime. His bright schoolboy face and the habit of wearing what looked like old army boots with his usual blue serge suit, made him a potential figure of fun, but he was a classical scholar and an able lawyer. For the rank and file of the party, he was once the epitome of true Conservatism; which he defined as the necessity for continuity in social and political life, the importance of a proper balance between social cohesion and personal liberty, and a connexion between religious belief – he was a pious and reflective Anglican – and social stability.

By the seventies, Hailsham was convinced that our economic troubles were symptoms and not causes of Britain's decline, and that a major cause was the supremacy of Parliament. Too many people, he concluded, had forgotten that it was only one of Dicey's two great principles of the British constitution. The other was the rule of law, and Common Law could be as effective as a written constitution. Parliamentary supremacy had nevertheless taken precedence because of the claims that the Commons represented the people, was the embodiment of freedom and could bring about the greater happiness for the majority. It had not turned out that way, and the choice today was between parliamentary dictatorship and a democratic system which could come to terms with right and wrong. Cicero, Hailsham added, had said that man had a natural propensity to love his fellow men, and this was the basis of law.

*

I could understand why Hailsham was dismissed as an anachronism. The Labour Left talked about social justice and the new Tories about incentives. Both were abstractions but fashionable, unlike sentiments such as a man's natural propensity to love. He was one of the last lingering shadows of a past long forgotten at Westminster, and one had to look elsewhere for a countervailing force to the transient majority and parliamentary dictatorship.

One man who thought that he could deal effectively with both was David Steel, the leader of the Liberal party. We met in his office in the House of Commons, a narrow cluttered room which the most junior American Congressman would have rejected as utterly inadequate. He was shrewd and level-headed, superior to the flat-vowelled image which was occasionally allowed to appear on television screens. Steel had been dismissed as the Boy David because he looked young for his years, but the sneer had a deeper meaning. He was in fact fighting two Goliaths, the Labour and

31

Conservative parties, and he believed that proportional representation was the best shot in his sling.

Election arithmetic provided the proof. The Liberals won 13.8 per cent of the vote in the 1979 general election but only 11 seats. With PR they could have won 87 seats, and with that many seats could have held the balance of power in this and probably future Parliaments. They could hope to diminish the danger of the transient majority and keep the parliamentary dictatorship of the governing party within bounds. They could join a coalition, or negotiate a pact as they did with Labour in the late seventies, or by simply remaining an opposition party upon whose support the government had to depend. In other words, Steel believed that PR could be a countervailing force almost as effective as the checks and balances of a written constitution.

Steel was convinced that the concentration of power within the Cabinet and the over-centralization of government had contributed to Britain's decline. He said that Britain must be the most over-centralized democratic country in the world. America had its states, West Germany its Länder, and even France its prefectures. Hans-Dietrich Genscher, his opposite number in West Germany, had told him that he would always be grateful for what Britain did for his country after the second world war. We had given them proportional representation, decentralized government and a modern trade union system.

We did indeed, and it must help to explain why West Germany, with little experience, has become one of the more successful and efficient industrial democracies. Proportional representation as practised there disciplines the two major parties and effectively denies seats in the Bundestag to extremist parties. Neither the Social Democrats nor the Christian Democrats are generally strong enough to form a government alone, and the coalition partner of each party has invariably been the Free Democrats, the liberal party. According to Steel, Helmut Schmidt, the Chancellor, was grateful to the Free Democrats because they had helped him to control the extremists of his own Social Democratic party.

Multi-party systems can of course lack stability and direction, but Steel said that the concept of two monolithic classes represented by the two major parties was more dangerous. Nevertheless, the two-party system was still widely supported. He recalled that when he first won the border constituency of Roxburgh, Selkirk and Peebles by defeating the sitting Tory Member, the wife of the Labour candidate tearfully accused him of dividing the progressive vote. She could not understand that Britain was not divided into two opposing classes, that many Britons preferred the middle ground.

There were of course reasons other than class for supporting one of the two major parties. Even the discontented were loth to waste their votes on a party with small hope of winning, but Steel said that confrontation politics had only brought about economic and social decline. It was time to try a different pattern of government, one based upon the consent of the broad majority of the electorate. That alone could provide the basis for the long-term programme of reform so urgently needed in Britain. He claimed that the Lib-Lab pact had shown what could be done. Its achievements were limited because it was an experiment, but during the short life of the pact the Labour government was required to respect the views of the majority. Certainly the divisive policies of Labour's lunatic left were held in check.

It is possible that Callaghan was as grateful as Schmidt for the help received in controlling his extremists, but neither the Conservative nor the Labour party is likely to introduce proportional representation willingly. The Liberals know this; their 1979 election manifesto said that both parties shared a vested interest in the preservation of Britain's divided society. The unrepresentative nature of the electoral system protected them, and continuing industrial and social confrontation re-enforced their links with opposing sides of industry. Britain's secretive and centralized structure of government also protected them, turn and turn about, from Parliament and public. Many leaders of both parties would rather see Britain's economy drift further behind our continental neighbours, and accept another cycle of industrial conflict and popular discontent, than change the pattern of adversary politics which supports their alternating hold on political power.

That said, PR is likely to be introduced only if enough voters break the habits and prejudice of a lifetime and vote for third parties. The evidence is not encouraging although the number of third parties has increased in recent years. Apart from the Liberals, United Ulster Unionists and Communists, they include the Scottish National Party, Plaid Cymru, the Workers' Revolutionary Party and the National Front. The combined Labour and Conservative share of the vote dropped from 89.4 percent in 1970 to 75.4 percent in February 1974, and to 75.1 percent in October of that year. In 1979 it rose to 80.8 percent, but was still well below that for any other post-war election, when the average was 92.0 percent.

Dissatisfaction with Westminster has encouraged support for other reforms. Devolution could relieve pressure on Parliament and reduce centralization. The first attempt failed largely because the Scotland and Wales Acts were the products of political expediency and not principled belief in constitutional reform. They were drafted to ensure the continued existence of the then Labour government and not as a first step towards decentralization. The referendum, as used in Switzerland and many American states, could adjust the balance of power between the people and Parliament. It is a blunt instrument, and in Switzerland has tended to favour the forces of reaction. There is also no guarantee that Parliament would accept the result of a referendum as final. The Labour left still refuses to accept the European referendum.

*

The idea that citizens must be defended against Parliament is, I suppose, too novel for many people to accept. After all, Parliament is supposed to represent the people and to defend and promote their interests. Most of us would like to believe this, but the 1979 Liberal manifesto's version of what goes on in Parliament was closer to the truth than we are prepared to admit. The European referendum is a case in point. It was first promoted by Tony Benn in the belief that the electorate would vote against British entry into the EEC. He was proved wrong, but instead of accepting the result as the will of the people, he chose to believe that they had been manipulated by the media, and decided that we, the people, could not be trusted to make up our own minds.

Such is the level of arrogance the supremacy of Parliament admits and even nurtures. Nevertheless, a growing minority of Members are becoming uneasy and believe that Parliament must be reformed; that the executive and bureaucracy must be made more accountable, that the quality of legislation must be improved, and that backbenchers must be allowed to play a more useful role.

Part of the evidence was in the proposal to the Select Committee on Procedure to increase the number and scope of parliamentary committees. In its first report, published in 1978, the committee recommended the establishment of new committees to scrutinize the activities of the public service on a continuing and systematic basis. The areas chosen were Agriculture, Defence, Education, Science and Arts, Energy, Environment, Foreign Affairs, Home Affairs, Industry and Employment, Social Services, Trade and Consumer Affairs, Transport, and the Treasury.

At first the proposal was not welcomed by party leaders, and sternly opposed by Michael Foot and Enoch Powell. They defended the existing system and then acknowledged that it was no longer working well. Both men were romantics, and believed

34

that good government was best served in the cut and thrust of debate on the floor of the House, and not by Members hobnobbing in committee rooms. They were not alone in remembering the great debates held down through the centuries, but times had changed. The parliamentary contest had become too unequal and life outside too complicated; and the two great parliamentarians eventually agreed that the time for reform was ripe.

At first sight this modest reform did not promise the dawn of a new democratic age. It was tried, if half-heartedly, in the sixties when Crossman set up a few specialist committees, and they were allowed to fade quietly away. Cynics suggested that the reform was acceptable to Ministers this time because they believed that the committees would keep awkward Members occupied and reduce rather than increase the efforts of backbenchers to control the executive. Their cynicism could be unfounded; for instance, Healey believed that the latest generation of backbenchers realized that they had only one chance in three of joining the government, and many were no longer prepared to toe the party line in the hope of advancement. They might seek careers as committee chairmen, as did many American Congressmen.

Congressional committees are of course well established and powerful. They and not the executive branch draft legislation. The White House sends a message up to Congress, and the appropriate committees in the House of Representatives and the Senate hear testimony and mark up their own Bills. The differences are settled in conference, and the legislation eventually enacted is often very different from the proposals of the President. This is not always a good thing, and the committee system has often been abused, but the advantages are obvious. There is little or no secrecy; Congressmen belonging to the minority party can play a useful and fulfilling role, and effective oversight of the executive can be achieved. Bills are on the whole well drafted because of the time and thought devoted to them; and, most important in their eyes, the legislature and not the executive is the final arbiter. Even a presidential veto can be over-ruled.

We are unlikely to see such autonomous committees at Westminster in the foreseeable future, but those apprehensive of innovation should not oppose the reform on the grounds of historical and institutional continuity. As early as the sixteenth century, committees were regularly appointed at the beginning of each session of Parliament to consider election returns and matters of privilege, religion, griefs and petitions, trade and the courts of justice*. By the early seventeenth century the committees played an important part in the work of the House. Indeed, there is some similarity between those early Commons committees and the present American system, presumably because there was then more of a separation of powers in Britain than exists today. Certainly their development was stopped when the Monarch's representation in the House dwindled, and efforts were made to diminish the royal influence. The committees briefly flourished again in the nineteenth century, but thereafter restraints were imposed.

Arguably those restraints should be further relaxed now that the Prime Minister and Cabinet have inherited the divine right of kings. By playing a continuing watchdog role the committees could curb that unacceptable right without denying government the ability to govern. They could also help to achieve a measure of open government, which in the long run could be the greatest reform since newspapers were allowed unofficially to report parliamentary debates in the early nineteenth century. (It was finally made official in 1971).

Together with proportional representation and devolution, it could bring about a near-revolutionary change without the messy business of executing the Prime Minister of the day outside the Banqueting Hall in Whitehall – but it is unlikely to happen. When the committees were established in 1979, the Tory government made certain that they would have very little authority. They might be able to develop, but the two major parties remain determined to block any reform that could diminish their authority when in power. Parliament will almost certainly continue to swing from one ideological extreme to the other, and each swing will accelerate Britain's decline.

* *Parliament & Congress* by Kenneth Bradshaw and David Pring, Constable, London, 1972

THREE

Your Disobedient Servant

Thomas Jefferson once said that if he had to make a choice between government and newspapers he would take newspapers. He changed his mind when elected President, but this little anecdote sums up the dilemma for those who believe in open government. Mr. Jefferson – as we used to say over our mint juleps in Albemarle County, Virginia, as if he were still alive – was one of history's great democrats. His Declaration of Independence is a noble document. He was the intellectual descendent of Locke, and one of the first statesmen to see that democratic government depends upon the free flow of information. That said, he occasionally resented press intrusion when he came to power, and it can be argued that without official secrecy he could not have carried out his greatest coup, the Louisiana Purchase.

The problem, a clash of legitimate interests, remains with us today. I doubt that it will ever be resolved, but it is more of a problem in Britain than other democracies. I have worked in many of them as a foreign correspondent, and must report that journalists work under greater handicaps here than in, say, the United States, West Germany and other northern European countries. Without a doubt, one of the abiding weaknesses of the British people in general and their public men in particular is their love of secrecy.

The origins are respectable enough. The longing for privacy, and the respect for other people's privacy, is one of the British people's more endearing characteristics. It has a stabilizing influence on society, and helps to explain why London is a more civilized city to live in than New York; but its extension beyond the household and neighbourhood is less defensible.

Tocqueville was puzzled by the apparent contradiction of the British love of association and exclusion, and how both could be intimately combined. 'What better example of association than the union of individuals who form a club? What is more exclusive than the corporate personality represented by the club? The same applies to all civil and political associations.' And no more dramatically and damningly than in government and the Civil Service,

37

where the occasional need for discretion has become an almost impenetrable wall of silence.

For me, a journalist, the advantages of a free flow of information are obvious, but the importance I attach to more open government cannot be explained by narrow vocational interests. Indeed, I would personally regret the passing of the old order because it would deny me the opportunity to match my wits against Ministers, civil servants and others who occupy the high ground of authority. But so much for *machismo*; the public interest must come first, and there is no doubt in my mind that one of the grave weaknesses of the British system of government, and another reason for our decline, is the official craving for secrecy.

History helps to explain why. Bagehot wrote about Britain's deferential society, and he was undoubtedly right at the time. We had not been exposed to the American or French Revolution. We largely escaped 1848, and the old order continued more or less undisturbed and as exclusive as ever. Discontented and spirited Britons emigrated in their tens of thousands. More than half of my traceable forebears went to Canada and Australia. Most of those who stayed behind were cowed by traditional authority in the countryside and by the horrors of early industrialism in the towns. Parliament was very much a closed shop, and as already stated the press was not allowed to report debates until the early nineteenth century. Its power was therefore greatly restricted despite the gallant efforts and occasional successes of *The Times*. There was no place for the press in the official scheme of things. It had no rights. Journalists, except for one or two editors, were not respectable. They were regarded disparagingly as Grub Street scribblers or drunken bums. No doubt some of them were but no more than the politicians they reported.

The situation was wholly different in the United States. It was not a deferential society. Apart from the revolutionary generation, the British who came afterwards did not emigrate in coffin boats to be deferential, and they increased the suspicion of government which was always widespread. The press also saw itself as the nation's watchdog, and the First Amendment guaranteed its freedom. The separation of powers enlarged its function. The White House, Senate and House of Representatives were in effect in competition and each needed the press to communicate with the people, the source of all power.

Politics in the United States was never the special preserve of elites, despite the early prominence of those gentlemanly Virginians and morally-superior Bostonians. Ordinary Americans expected to participate. Andrew Jackson created the world's first mass political party when the Tories and Whigs at Westminster were little more than parliamentary factions. For these and other reasons the press was seen as an essential part of the political process at all levels.

Britain is no longer a deferential society, and relations between Parliament and the press are better than they were. Ministers and backbenchers can be informative when it suits their purpose. Senior civil servants can be helpful as long as they are not quoted. A few of their politicized juniors have been known to leak important documents, but as an institution government is still wedded to secrecy despite the Labour party's 1974 manifesto which favoured more public access to official information. They changed their mind after returning to office and little progress had been made when Parliament was dissolved five years later. The new Tory government was not prepared to be party to such liberal nonsense and tried to put the clock back, with the Protection of Information Bill. This ignored changes in British society and the very basis of democracy and gave Ministers and civil servants virtually unlimited discretion and decision-making authority without rendering them accountable. It would have been a grave threat to the freedom of the press by restricting its ability to investigate and report on subjects of legitimate and significant public concern.

The Bill was withdrawn because of the Blunt affair which proved that officials had withheld information from their elected lords and masters; in this instance Lord Home when he was Prime Minister. Anthony Blunt, a distinguished art historian, spied for the Russians and helped two other traitors, Guy Burgess and Donald Maclean, to escape to the Soviet Union. He confessed in exchange for immunity in 1964, and his treachery would not have been revealed without the public access to the National Archives in Washington granted by the American Freedom of Information Act. Andrew Boyle, whose book, *The Climate of Treason*, led to the exposure of Blunt, acknowledged the debt he owed to Washington, and the realization that his book could not have been published if the Protection of Information Bill had been enacted forced the Tory government to change its mind.

The position was still unsatisfactory at the time of writing although there was no legitimate excuse for such authoritarian secrecy. Except in sensitive areas such as defence, secrecy makes for bad government as well as offends the spirit of democracy. It also assumes that a handful of Ministers and their civil servants have cornered the nation's wisdom, which is offensive nonsense.

The fact of the matter is that most of them are afraid of a free flow of information. That is not an exaggeration; I have seen fear and apprehension in their eyes too often to be persuaded otherwise. They are afraid because a large measure of secrecy is essential for the survival of any establishment, Tory or Labour, political or official. It enhances the mystique of government, gives an unfair advantage to those with access, maintains privilege, and prevents the exposure of inefficiency and corruption. A free flow of information would wash most of that away. It could also be a revolutionary force, which helps to explain why the American revolutionaries gave the press constitutional protection. The US Constitution could not have been ratified without the Bill of Rights, and reluctant states might not have been persuaded to join the Union without the cogent arguments publicized in *The Federalist*.

This fear explains the formidable legislation enacted at Westminster to ensure that secrecy is maintained. The various Official Secrets Acts provide many exceptions to normal criminal procedure, such as wider powers of arrest, a reduction of the prosecution's burden of proof, exceptions to the rules of evidence, the possibility of hearings in camera and heavy sentences. The law of contempt is also misused to defend the indefensible, and as a consequence we are a half-free nation unable to deal with some of the causes of our decline.

Bagehot recognized that the Cabinet depended upon secrecy for much of its unique authority and secrecy has also increased the power of the Civil Service. There is a strong argument that it is now too powerful. The Eleventh Report of the Commons' Expenditure Committee, published in 1977, said that the resolution of the struggle for power between the Cabinet and the bureaucracy on the one hand and between the Cabinet and Parliament on the other was the central issue of our age. Top civil servants misconceived their role in society. They came into the Service with what Balliol men used to refer to as the unconscious realization of effortless superiority although they were almost completely lacking in experience. They had invented for themselves the role of governing the country, and saw themselves as politicians writ large. They sought to govern the country according to their own narrow interests, education and background, none of which fitted them to govern a modern technological, industrialized, pluralist and urbanized society.

'They can and do relegate Ministers to the second division (appropriately enough they call their own union the First Division) through a variety of devices. They include delay, which is a potent one when governments are in a minority situation or coming to the end of their political life; foreclosing options through official committees which parallel both Cabinet sub-committees and a host of other ministerial committees; interpreting minutes and policy decisions in ways not wholly intended;

slanting statistics, giving Ministers insufficient time to take decisions: taking advantage of Cabinet splits and politically-divided ministerial teams; and even going behind Ministers' backs to other ministries and other Ministers . . . . In doing all these things they act in what they conceive to be the public good . . . . (but) they are arrogating to themselves power that properly belongs to the people and their representatives.'

The report also alleged three biases in recruitment: a preference for Oxbridge graduates, for former public schoolboys, and for arts rather than social and natural science graduates. The bias, at least in a statistical sense, was admitted by the then head of the Home Civil Service. He could hardly do otherwise because Oxbridge provided almost 60 percent of recruits in 1976, although he did make the point that high flyers tended to go to Oxford and Cambridge and the Civil Service naturally sought to recruit the most able graduates. The report also said that Ministers rejected the claim that civil servants existed solely to serve the government of the day, and that they took their policy instructions from the Minister. Departments were reluctant to change their views to meet the policy of new Ministers, and when they did submit they tried to reinstate their own policies as time passed and the Minister's political will weakened. Some Departments were so large that they could apply their own policies without the Minister's knowledge.

These are serious allegations, which in effect charge the Civil Service with manning an invisible government as the Central Intelligence Agency was supposed to have done in the United States before the Watergate revelations. Indeed, they are more serious because investigation established that American Presidents were directly responsible for CIA operations, at least in broad outline, while British Ministers are said to be either ignored or resisted. In other words, a closed shop of middle-class mandarins, unaccountable except to themselves, runs the country largely for the benefit of their narrow class interests. If only half true, it would be unconstitutional and would certainly help to explain Britain's decline.

*

Most senior civil servants have a passion for anonymity, but the Permanent Secretary who sat opposite me at lunch one day would have stood out in any gathering. A handsome man, his face was all the more impressive because of its calmness. The lively but steady eyes suggested great self-confidence and natural authority. He could have been a youngish general or admiral but for the clerical grey suit and Oxbridge college tie. Much of this could no doubt be explained by his social background, slightly aristocratic and very good schools, but there was something more. He had spent more years than he probably cared to remember at the centre of power.

Yet it emerged that his self-confidence was not complete. The Expenditure Committee might have thought with good reason that he and his like had too much power, but he knew that he could never be ultimately responsible. He could advise but the Minister would always be responsible, which was why some of his colleagues had left the Service. They could not accept the denial of final authority. There were compensations of course. He had become a civil servant because he had been taught to regard public service as one of the highest fields of human endeavour. Then there was the variety, and the company was congenial – presumably because of those biases in recruitment policy. He had been among his own from the beginning.

The Permanent Secretary said that he had learned to accept the constitutional position, although apparently it rankled occasionally, as he had learned to accept the passing of empire. Its passing had nevertheless had a deleterious effect in more ways than one. The spirit and pride as well as the power and influence of Britain had been diminished. Even ordinary working people once gloried in the empire, and the country's leadership had been given a sense of purpose. We tended to forget, he said, what it had been like to be responsible for literally hundreds of millions of people all over the world. Now, if anybody thought of the past, there was only guilt or ridicule. The empire had also been a fount of leaders, and that had dried up. There were now no natural leaders, although he acknowledged that leadership was much more difficult with an educated electorate. One could only hope to persuade.

He admitted to a deepening sense of pessimism. Too many opportunities had been missed. North Sea oil was God's gift, and we had already wasted the first few years. He did not believe that Britain had gone down the drain, but it would if we did not pull ourselves together within the next ten years. It was difficult to see how, government was now very complicated and Parliament was no longer a suitable instrument. The adversary system had not worked well since the main parties had become ideological. The legislative load was too heavy for Parliament and the Civil Service. There was no countervailing force. Backbenchers should become watchdogs of the executive; there should be more American-style committees.

We finished our coffee and walked out of the club to the waiting official car. The pessimism had gone. The dark eyes were lively again as we said goodbye, and for a moment I was reminded of the world of Graham Greene where men such as the Permanent Sec-

42

retary disposed of the nation's business in the coffee rooms of Pall Mall clubs. His like wielded considerable power, but not necessarily because they went to the right schools, fought in the best regiments and belonged to exclusive clubs. Many of his colleagues had what was once known as humble beginnings. They had won scholarships and excelled in examinations; they had been accepted by the more traditional mandarins as Indians had been accepted as equals in the old Indian Civil Service. Individually and collectively they had been of small account until the growth and centralization of government, administration and the welfare state, a combination which could not be controlled and directed by Ministers.

The rate of growth would have astounded Northcote and Trevelyan, whose 1853 Report established what we now know as the Home Civil Service. At that time the public service employed 75,000 people, most of them in the Post Office and Customs and Excise. The officials and clerks who manned the central government departments numbered only about 1,700. In the late seventies the Civil Service employed nearly 750,000. The Quangos, quasi-autonomous non-government organizations, employed a further 184,000. Total government expenditure, including the nationalized sector, rose from £4,582 million in 1946 to about £60,000 million in the late seventies.

In organizational terms we were well on our way to becoming a socialist or fascist state. This was not the result of empire-building, at least not most of it, or of some sinister conspiracy of the mandarins. It was the will of Parliament, the consequence of all those laws enacted over the years. Churchill, Macmillan and Home were as much responsible as Attlee, Wilson and Callaghan. A similar growth had occurred in all industrial democracies, including the United States where the expansion of the federal bureaucracy had more than kept pace with the growth of federal power.

In the early years of the American republic, suspicion of government prevented the establishment of a permanent civil service. The Jacksonian assumption that any citizen was fit to run the country led to the spoils system, inefficiency and corruption, and a permanent service was eventually established in 1883. The top jobs are still reserved for political appointees, and in recent years many have been filled by in-and-outers, that is by men who move in and out of government. Most of them have been lawyers and academics content to return to their practices and campuses between tours of duty. The system has its advantages, but it has not improved the Civil Service which tends to be more bureaucratic than in Britain because their temporary bosses do not stay long enough to get a grip on their departments.

The British Civil Service was also established to do away with nepotism, incompetence and other defects inherited from the eighteenth century. The Northcote-Trevelyan Report proposed the introduction of competitive entry examinations for university graduates, and the tradition of the all-rounder emerged over the years. In the words of the Fulton Report*, the gifted layman moving frequently from job to job within the Service, could once take a practical view of any problem, irrespective of its subject matter. The system worked well enough when government was small, but, Fulton concluded, now had most damaging consequences. They had obviously compounded the weakness of big government.

The complexity of modern government was well described in Fulton. 'Its traditional regulatory functions have multiplied in size and greatly broadened in scope. It has taken on vast new responsibilities. It is expected to achieve such general economic aims as full employment, a satisfactory rate of growth, stable prices and a healthy balance of payments. Through these and other policies (e.g. public purchasing, investment grants, financial regulators) it profoundly influences the output, costs and profitability of industry generally in both the home and overseas markets. Through nationalization it more directly controls a number of basic industries. It has responsibilities for the location of industry and for town and country planning. It engages in research and development both for civil and military purposes. It provides comprehensive social services and is now expected to promote the fullest possible development of individual human potential. All these changes have made for massive growth in public expenditure. Public spending means public control. A century ago the tasks of government were mainly passive and regulatory. Now they amount to a much more active and positive engagement in our affairs.

'Technological progress and the vast amount of new knowledge have made a major impact on these tasks and on the process of taking decisions; the change goes on. Siting a new airport, buying military supplies, striking the right balance between coal, gas, oil and nuclear-powered electricity in a new energy policy – all these problems compel civil servants to use new techniques of analysis, management and coordination which are beyond those not especially trained in them.'

That means the vast majority of the men and women in the higher reaches of the Civil Service. No wonder the Treasury has rarely if ever managed to get its economic and financial forecasts and policies right. Fulton recommended a number of reforms, but

* *The Civil Service*, HMSO, 1968

ten years later few of them had been implemented. Lord Crowther-Hunt, who was a member of the Fulton Committee, said, 'In general, the Civil Service implemented those parts of Fulton that it liked and added to its power, and failed to implement the ideas that would have made it more professional and more accountable to Parliament and the public.'

The inadequacy of the Civil Service must therefore be seen as another reason for Britain's decline in that it remains essentially a nineteenth century service largely incapable of planning and administering programmes enacted by post-war Parliaments to modernize, change and improve British life and industry. The first responsibility rests with Westminster which apparently believes that passing legislation is rather like waving a magic wand. Its intentions are apparently thought to have been realized once the Royal Assent has been given. Certainly too much importance is attached to administrative solutions. More often than not, new governments reorganize one or more of the great departments in the belief that beneficial change will follow.

That said, arguably no Civil Service can do much better after the centralization of government and administration, and the nationalization of industry, have passed a certain level. This is surely one reason why the Soviet Union and other so-called socialist countries are inefficient as well as repressive. The very nature of bureaucracy makes for inertia and resistance to change. David Owen, the former Foreign Secretary who also served as a Minister in the Department of Health and Social Services, said that bureaucracy was the enemy of radicalism, and he did not speak from the left wing of the Labour party. 'I am never told what I can do, but what I can't do.'

He added that a radical politician could not expect support from the Civil Service; not that officials conspired to prevent change, it was just the inertia built into the system. He and his ministerial colleagues had discovered that it was almost impossible to get a prompt decision because Whitehall was committee-bound. And when inertia was overcome by political will and change was brought about, the results in administrative terms could be disastrous.

Neither the Fulton Committee on the Civil Service nor the Expenditure Committee criticized the men and women who served it. The loyalty, dedication and hard work of the majority were generously acknowledged. There can be no argument about that, but it does seem to conflict with the charge that the Civil Service is a kind of invisible government largely accountable only to itself. If it does run the country according to its own lights and interests how can it be loyal to the Ministers it is supposed to serve?

*

Every Permanent Secretary would deny the charge of disloyalty, some with indignation and others with weary resignation. Certainly it cannot be assumed that they are natural Tories and defenders of the *status quo* because of their Oxbridge background. Many civil servants vote Labour, and probably prefer Labour governments because socialism means centralization and more job opportunities and power and influence for the Civil Service.

Certainly most of them, whatever party they vote for, respond to Ministers who provide leadership; in other words, a strong Minister can generally depend upon the enthusiasm, loyalty and support of his civil servants as a strong divisional commander can depend upon his brigadiers.

That said, senior civil servants do belong to a very small and powerful elite. Fulton reported that there were less than 3,000 in the Administrative Class. Their numbers have since increased, but they still have a common sense of purpose and *esprit de corps*. The old Indian Civil Service regarded itself as the iron frame which kept the Indian Empire together, and while the top men and women in the Home Civil Service are not given to such dramatic claims, they know that they are indispensable. They insist that they take their policy instructions from the Minister. That said, their most important function is to advise him. They influence in varying degree the policy they implement in the name of the Minister, and a weak Minister with a strong Permanent Secretary is little more than a rubber stamp. They also claim that it is not their function to prevent the worst excesses of the left or right, but they also have the right of appeal to the Prime Minister if they consider that their own Minister has acted improperly.

Civil servants are clearly not political eunuchs, and I would suggest that only unthinking populists would have it otherwise. Few Ministers have in fact complained of disloyal or resisting civil servants. Crossman did not get on with Dame Evelyn Sharp, his Permanent Secretary at the Ministry of Housing and Local Government, but he admired her. He wrote in his Diaries, 'She is rather like Beatrice Webb in her attitude to life, to the Left in the sense of wanting improvement and social justice quite passionately and yet a tremendous patrician and utterly contemptuous and arrogant. . .' Some readers of the Diaries might have concluded that was a fair description of Crossman, but the power of the Civil Service was evident when he sought to replace her. Crossman wanted one man and the then Head of the Home Civil Service another. Crossman wrote, 'He said I must

46

appreciate that a Permanent Secretary would last longer than a Minister and that therefore he was concerned to find one who not only got on with me but who was suitable for the Department.'

That was only the beginning. As Anthony Howard noted in his introduction to the condensed version of the Diaries*, Crossman was genuinely astonished when he realized the full extent of the power of the Civil Service. The power rested on two time-honoured Whitehall customs, the first being its role as keeper of the muniments. 'The fact that, through the Cabinet Secretariat, the Civil Service not merely records the discussions of Cabinet but also minutes its decisions, bestows on permanent officials a tremendous discretionary prerogative. Only what is recorded officially ranks as precedent: and, therefore, precedent very soon becomes that to which the Civil Service – and in particular the Cabinet Secretariat – gives its approval.'

The second shock for Crossman was the ease with which Permanent Secretaries combined to impose what was called the official view. This was done at two levels. First, there was the official advice a Minister got within his own Department; secondly, there was always a cohesive, inter-departmental view pressed upon the Minister's colleagues when any disputed question was referred to the Cabinet. This was achieved by a network of official committees similar to the Cabinet committees: Defence and Foreign Affairs, Home Affairs, Economic Development and the like. According to Crossman, 'Very often the whole job is pre-cooked in the official committee to a point from which it is extremely difficult to reach any other conclusion than that already determined by the officials in advance; and if agreement is reached at the lower level of a Cabinet committee, only formal approval is needed from the full Cabinet. This is the way in which Whitehall ensures that the Cabinet system is relatively harmless.'

Crossman was not the first to discover the alleged invisible government in Whitehall. The late John Mackintosh† suggested that it would only cause alarm if one assumed that no official should exercise any element of discretion. Once the assumption was cast aside, the argument that government had fallen into the hands of civil servants merely demonstrated that policy was made at all levels. There was no cause for anxiety while Ministers created the appropriate atmosphere in administration, encouraged certain schemes and restrained others and, on occasion, introduced into the thinking of departments changes of direction and emphasis. Mackintosh recognized the obvious dangers of official committees preempting Cabinet committees, but added that the

* Hamish Hamilton and Jonathan Cape, 1979
† *The British Cabinet*. Stevens, 1962

arrangements and attitudes of the Civil Service were usually accepted by leaders of the major parties, especially after they had had experience of office. They realized that government without a stream of suggestions and comment would be totally impossible.

I am on balance less complacent than was Mackintosh about the role of the Civil Service, although I accept that without its active participation in policy making government might well be impossible. Violent swings of the ideological pendulum would have been even more damaging to the national interest if those departmental philosophies and points of view had not applied a brake of sorts. We must accept the Civil Service as a powerful and vital component of government even if the Permanent Secretaries are not elected, but I cannot accept that they and other civil servants should remain unaccountable.

There can be no doubt that this is the case. Sir John Hunt, who as the Secretary of the Cabinet, was the most powerful man in the Civil Service, admitted as much when testifying before the Commons' Expenditure Committee. He said that the concept of Ministerial responsibility had been modified since the growth of big government, a Minister could not be expected to resign because of a mistake made by a civil servant he had never heard of. In other words, civil servants do act without reference to the Minister. This is no doubt necessary; as Mackintosh noted, a Minister probably deals regularly with a dozen senior officials but he cannot know and watch over dozens of Assistant Secretaries who nominally work under his supervision. Hunt and Mackintosh failed, however, to acknowledge the consequences. Both recognized that civil servants had made mistakes over the years, many damaging and expensive for the nation, but very few had been held accountable. The number of resignations is statistically insignificant.

This, if you like, is the unacceptable face of the Civil Service. I would be required to resign if I was guilty of errors of judgement damaging or embarrassing to *The Times,* as would executives of most companies. No wonder Britain is in a mess when the Civil Service, which controls, directs or influences about half of the country's endeavours, cannot be held responsible for its mistakes and failures.

Suggestions that they should be made accountable have been successfully resisted, and many ingenious defences have been erected. The basic defence is that no official would express his honest opinion in a minute if he knew that it would be available to the public sooner than the present 30-year rule of silence and secrecy. This is assumed to be an eternal truth, but why? Another line of defence is still the hoary untruth that civil servants are accountable to Ministers. A third is that they would be politicized if they lost their anonymity. I can understand why they cling to anonymity, it must make for a quiet life, but there is much more at stake than the comfort and future job prospects of civil servants. We have come back to the Jeffersonian dilemma confronting those who believe, indeed know, that open government makes for better government.

After comparisons with other industrial democracies, it is clear, if not to civil servants, Ministers and politicians who hope to succeed them, that there is an undeniable case for increasing the flow of information. I am not suggesting that we should have a Freedom of Information Act on the American model, but the Official Secrets Act must be liberalized and not replaced with more repressive legislation. The Act made absolute the convention of Ministerial responsibility, although no Minister has resigned since Crichel Down in 1954, and is now a nefarious smokescreen to hide inefficiency, impropriety and wrong-doing.

*

The case for a more open government, I am not suggesting a completely open government, should not have to be restated. After all, public debate is supposed to be an essential part of political democracy, and there can be no real debate without access to official information. Parliament cannot carry out its watchdog role without access. Effective legislation cannot be drafted and sensibly debated, and the Civil Service cannot be made accountable and more efficient, without the free flow of information. I am not suggesting that more open government is the panacea for Britain's many problems, but it would help. The only argument is where the line is to be drawn between the openness required for efficient government and the secrecy or discretion required for the defence of the realm, certain economic decisions, business secrets, and last, but not least, the confidences of citizens. There is also the question of priority; who has the greater right to information, Parliament, the press, pressure groups or individuals?

The first priority unquestionably belongs to Parliament, and the best conduit should be the new select committees. Certainly Question Time is inadequate. The scope of the new committees is restricted because of the conflict between the objectives of parliamentary oversight and political partisanship, but there is little hope of achieving a more open government without an extension of the system. Certainly, the responsibilities of the committees should not be confined to oversight. It would be nice to know what went wrong after the event, but Parliament, if it is to function usefully, must have information before and during the legislative phases. The Public Accounts Committee was already moving in that direction, and Edward du Cann said in 1979 that the committee could restore parliamentary control over the volume of public expenditure.

Committee hearings, whether or not they are open to the press, nearly always raise the question of security. One Labour Minister was worried about some Members who he believed could not be trusted. He not only assumed that a Minister or a backbencher might again be foolish enough to share a mistress with a Soviet military attaché, but was particularly wary of a few members of his own party whom he loosely labelled as Trots. He was convinced that they would take any sensitive information to their favourite eastern European embassy.

The Defence Committee would obviously have to be careful, but Parliament deserves more information than is now given in Defence White Papers. The Defence Department in Washington, which has much more to be secretive about, provides Congress with a hundred times more information, and its annual policy statement, which gives the strength of the armed services and discusses nuclear strategy, is freely available to journalists, including foreign correspondents. In any case, if Ministers cannot trust their own backbenchers they should say so publicly rather than use potential treason as an excuse for secrecy.

Certainly the government and Civil Service should not deny information essential for efficient decision-making. The average American Congressman is by nature more talkative than a British backbencher, and the flow of information from Capitol Hill can reach flood proportions but the Republic remains as secure as ever. Nowadays, there are even committees overseeing the intelligence agencies and, much more important, the federal budget. Britain's new committees could do much to open up government, improve the quality of debate, cut waste and hold Ministers and civil servants accountable.

The press could also make a contribution if civil servants could be persuaded or required to cooperate. At one time they regarded journalists as enemies, as well as drunken bums. I can recall asking the British embassy in Beirut in the fifties to help me get a visa for Iraq. I only wanted a letter confirming that I worked for *The Times*, and was known to the embassy, a common practice with other embassies and their nationals, but it was refused. I was told that it was not a function of a British embassy to help British correspondents.

Whitehall has since dragged itself into the twentieth century, and the Departments now have large information sections. They can be helpful, but they exist to sell the policies of their Ministers and the service provided is inevitably suspect or inadequate. Certainly it is not the service I was accustomed to in foreign capitals. I can recall seeking information in Bonn about the support costs West Germany paid towards the upkeep of the British Army of the Rhine. It was a politically sensitive subject largely because the West Germans did not want to pay more and relations between the two governments had deteriorated, but a Dr. Esse in the Economics Ministry regularly provided me with all the facts and figures I required.

The present situation can be ludicrous. Information denied to the British press is often automatically shared with friendly allied governments, and Fleet Street newspapers now ask their Washington offices to file information which at home is still treated as secret. This trans-Atlantic traffic has measurably increased since Congress passed the Freedom of Information Act. Even faceless civil servants do not want to appear ludicrous, and Whitehall has relented a little. Another reason is that the demand for more open government can no longer be ignored, and before Mrs. Thatcher became Prime Minister, a decision had obviously been made to disarm critics if not meet half way the legitimate requirements of the press.

Relations with the government are satisfactory when the press plays the passive role of acting as a conduit for official information, but not when it tries to report what has now become to be known as the decision-making process. The need for more public information at this stage is beyond dispute. The public is not informed when only informed of an accomplished fact. The democratic process is diminished. This was reluctantly recognized in the sixties when Green Papers were introduced, but they do not go far enough. To do their job properly, journalists need the basic papers because policy options can be dropped before a Green Paper is drafted, and in any case some Green Papers look very white.

Journalists also need to talk to officials as well as Ministers, and some of them do after they have established a working relationship. The posh ones take their official contacts to lunch at their clubs, the not-so-posh to the Savoy Grill, and ordinary working journalists can and do extract information in less costly circumstances, but civil servants are always aware of the Official Secrets Act and of the fact that their Ministers must on occasions put political considerations first. They are also said to be busy men, but so are their opposite numbers in Washington and Bonn where they and their political superiors always find time to see journalists. I regularly saw President Johnson alone, and his National Security Advisor and Secretary of State. Assistant Secretaries were available on the telephone, and I occasionally called at the Georgetown house of the Director of the Central Intelligence Agency for a drink.

They were cooperative not only because of the First Amendment; they talked to me because they regarded it as part of their job. They wanted to fuel the public debate, to influence me, or to fly a kite. They also regarded me as another source of information. The relationship was very grown-up, often politics at its sophisticated best, but of course they were not inhibited by an Official Secrets Act.

Clement Freud, the Liberal Member, managed to introduce a reforming Bill before Parliament was dissolved in 1979 but it was not enacted. I doubt that we shall achieve a greater flow of official information in the foreseeable future. Civil servants may not be quite so powerful as Crossman thought they were, but they have too many political allies to feel unduly threatened. The politicians also know that it is not a burning issue. Elections will not be lost because of their reluctance or refusal to be more open. Merlyn Rees, who as Home Secretary was supposed to have been responsible for fulfilling the Labour party's 1974 manifesto pledge, said that he was unlikely to find more than two or three of his constituents who were interested.

He was probably correct; as I have said, one of the abiding sins of the British people is their love of secrecy which they somehow equate with their respect for privacy. Nevertheless, they should realize that in an over-centralized welfare state a more open government is also necessary for apolitical citizens. Their rights can be overlooked, forgotten, ignored and even flouted by faceless civil servants at all levels. The very nature of bureaucracy makes for heartlessness and indifference as well as inefficiency, waste and corruption.

As *The Guardian** said, 'Secrecy impinges on virtually every aspect of British life. Most citizens suffer from it, in one form or another. Either it immediately affects them, in their frustrated attempts to find out facts which have bearing upon their lives; or, in the longer term, it denies them the full information to which they are entitled about the performance of their government, information which they need to make an informed choice at election times. People are being denied information which should be their right. Claimants are not allowed to see the codes governing the administration of benefits and are therefore not able to judge or challenge the exercise of official discretion in interpreting the law. A passenger about to embark on a cruise liner cannot see reports which reveal whether the ship meets health standards. Motorists
* April 21, 1979

52

cannot, as they can in the United States, discover from Transport Ministry files whether a particular make of vehicle is defective. Citizens who wish to compare the record of their local authority with another in conserving and maintaining their historic buildings will be told by the Department of the Environment that such comparative material is confidential. The list is endless . . .'

That leading article was published many years after authority – government, Parliament and the Civil Service – was forced to accept that while Britons should consider themselves fortunate to live in this sceptred isle and seat of majesty, it was necessary to import the idea of an Ombudsman from Scandinavia. The Parliamentary Commissioner for Administration, as he is officially known, was not, however, given the powers of a real Ombudsman. His jurisdiction was limited to reported cases of injustice caused by maladministration although his opposite numbers in Sweden – and France – were empowered to help improve the system. In other words, while authority bent with the wind its roots remained firm in Westminster and Whitehall.

Once again the supremacy of Parliament prevented the country from making a modest advance in the footsteps of other more progressive countries. Party leaders were not prepared to accept even a slight diminution of their authority. Few backbenchers were willing to see their own efforts to protect and help constituents overshadowed by a more effective arrangement. It mattered not that many people would suffer or be frustrated, parliamentary supremacy had to be maintained.

FOUR

This Great Movement of Ours

Bagehot knew that his cozy but effective Parliament would be doomed once universal suffrage was introduced, and it was eventually killed by the Labour party. The Conservatives and Liberals were quick to recognize the significance of the mass vote after the last Reform Bill, and sought to organize it, but Labour was the masses. It was to be led for many years by middle-class Oxbridge graduates, but it was a genuine working-class movement dedicated to social change and to the destruction of privilege which had created Bagehot's comfortable Parliament and their own blighted existence. Labour was to do more than change Westminster. It was to exploit the supremacy of Parliament to accelerate the process of centralization. Tocqueville's fears were to be fully realized, but Labour was not much influenced by Marx or continental radical movements in its early days.

Labour's two main characteristics were dissent and what perhaps can best be described as populism. Those Oxbridge intellectuals and the young angries from redbrick and white-tile universities who came after were often Marxists, but Labour can claim to be as British as the Conservative party and its old knights of the shires. Its roots are deep in our past. That past may not be recognized in boardrooms or the gin and Jaguar belt, but it is older than that of the Conservative party. Labour, as well as the trade unions, claims the Tolpuddle Martyrs as its own, but they were recent arrivals, and whatever the Tory press might think even some of the radical Left have a sturdy Britishness. Enoch Powell, the Tory maverick, once said to me that when he looked across the floor of the House to Tribunites such as Norman Atkinson and Eric Heffer he recognized them as true representatives of Britain.

Some of the early ancestors of the Labour movement saw themselves as Saxons and Celts dominated by Normans, and their spirit could be expressed by Kipling's poem about the dying Norman knight warning his son to be careful when the Saxon peasant stood his ground and said that it was not right. I am not suggesting that the movement was founded in 1066 or soon after, although I think John Ball, who supported Wat Tyler at the time of the Peasants'

Revolt in 1381, spoke as a true Labour man when he asked, When Adam delved and Eve span who was then the gentleman? Others prefer to trace the party's origins back to the Puritans, Cromwell's New Model Army, the Levellers and the Diggers of the mid-seventeenth century. More recent ancestors were the Chartists of the nineteenth century and the trade union movement which established the party as we know it today.

The Levellers, a republican and democratic group active during the Interregnum of 1649–60, were the first to try to organize a recognizable political party. Their enemies labelled them as Levellers to suggest that they wanted to reduce men and women to one level, but they were in fact radical supporters of Parliament in whose name the Civil War had been fought. The Levellers wanted sovereignty to be transferred to the House of Commons, to the exclusion of the King and the Lords. Their other demands included manhood suffrage, the redistribution of parliamentary seats and annual or biennial elections; the decentralization of government; economic reform; equality before the law and law reform; the abolition of conscription, billeting, tithes and trading monopolies; freedom of worship and the disestablishment of the state church; security of tenure and the opening of enclosures. They also wanted to pull troops out of Ireland, which so enraged Oliver Cromwell that he shouted to the Council of State, If you do not break them they will break you.

They did nothing of the sort. The Levellers failed to capture the New Model Army and to win broad national support, perhaps because they were long before their time. Their programme could have been an early draft of the United States Constitution, which was written nearly 150 years later. Their modernity was also evident in pamphlets written by John Lilburne, William Walwyn and Richard Overton, which appealed to reason and the fundamentals of political theory although the population was still deferential to the squire and his relations. If they had survived they might well have been identified with the Social Democratic wing of the Labour party in that they appealed to small farmers, shopkeepers and artisans and not to the usual revolutionary fodder.

The Diggers were early agrarian communists, so called because they seized some uncultivated land and tried to farm it. (More than 300 years later another Diggers party was formed on the West Coast of the United States.) Gerrard Winstanley, their theoretician, wrote a blueprint for a communist society, and was probably responsible for pushing the Levellers to the right. Winstanley argued that the Civil War had been fought against the Norman power of king, landlords and priests, and that the common folk would not benefit until land was nationalized. Religion was the opium of the people and diverted men from asserting their rights on earth. The market economy was the cause of all oppression and war, the rich owed all their wealth to the poor, and a cooperative society was the only just society.

If the Levellers were the Social Democrats of the party, the Diggers were the Tribunites, and like Atkinson and Heffer represented something no less fundamental in the British character. Winstanley wrote that true freedom lies in the free enjoyment of the earth. Three hundred years later, my old mother could still remember a song with the refrain, Why should we be beggars with ballots in our hands when God gave the land to the people. Disturbing perhaps, and probably unpopular in modern Britain, but as British as the more recent respect for the Monarchy.

The early movements were often strongly religious and pacifist, and the Quakers were an obvious example. They were more interested in souls than ballots, but they were essentially democratic. They were pioneers in free education and worked for reform of the penal code and the prison system. They opposed slavery as early as 1670, and about one hundred years later petitioned Parliament to abolish it. They represented, if you like, the do-gooders in the movement. Religious non-conformity and the non-conformist conscience are still very much part of Labour's inheritance.

Other ancestors were the Chartists, who emerged as a political force when the Reform Bill of 1832 enfranchised the middle classes but not the workers. They acquired their name from the People's Charter, which demanded equal electoral areas, universal suffrage, salaries for Members of Parliament, no property qualifications, vote by ballot and annual Parliaments. Organized by the London Workingmen's Association, and helped by Tory factory reformers, the Chartists also had a militant wing dedicated to insurrection. About 3,000 men armed with guns and colliers' picks tried to capture Newport, Monmouthshire, but the operation was badly planned and many were killed and wounded in an ambush. The leaders were condemned to death, but were eventually transported to Australia.

This revolutionary spirit, especially strong in Wales and northern England, was fuelled by mass unemployment and the 1834 Poor Law which was seen as a capitalist plot to force them to work for starvation wages. Nevertheless, many Chartists had bourgeois ambitions. Their demand for social equality would be understood by many Labour voters today: That all shall have a good house to live in with a garden back or front, just as the occupier likes; good clothing to keep him warm and to make him look respectable, and plenty of good food and drink to make him look

56

and feel happy.

Chartism disappeared after the repeal of the Corn Law, Lord Shaftesbury's factory reforms and the transportation of many of their leaders. Others fled overseas, and one of them afterwards asked, Where are the armies of stalwart men that tramped over and changed the face of England? Transplanted, I fear, to other lands, cast out by England to build up Australia, New Zealand, Canada and, mainly the United States.

Among them were William Carnegie, whose son Andrew was the great ironmaster and philanthropist, and Matthew Trumbull who became a general in the American army. The son of a third was imprisoned for life for the part he played in Chicago's Haymarket riots. Their arrival in the United States caused some disquiet because they were seen as part of an international conspiracy to suborn American democracy, but Britain's loss was America's gain. They had a catalytic impact upon the American labour movement, out of all proportion to their numbers, while in Britain the loss of so many vigorous working-class leaders hindered the general development of the trade union movement for the next forty years.*

*

Ronald Hayward, the general secretary of the Labour party, said that he was a Cotswold peasant, and the soft voice was convincing although his office was as large as any corporate suite. It was all the more impressive because the party's headquarters was still in Transport House, Smith Square, a smallish building and the headquarters of the Transport and General Workers Union. It also housed a branch of the Cooperative Bank. The party was in fact a tenant of the Transport and General until it moved to offices south of the Thames, and given the shortage of space Hayward's office was enormous. He sat beneath a life-size portrait of Clem Attlee, and other portraits of the party's great lined the other walls. It could have been the boardroom of a large company except for the homeliness of Ron, as he preferred to be known. He sat sucking his pipe and sipping tea, a combined pastime of many Labour people, exuding the proletarian friendliness also common with the movement.

Hayward, a Methodist, was strongly influenced by some Welsh miners who worked in a quarry near his village during the Depression. He was only sixteen when he joined the party before serving in the Royal Air Force during the war, and was afterwards offered a place at Ruskin College. It must have been tempting for a

* *British Chartists in America*. Ray Boston. Manchester University Press 1971

cabinet-maker with political ambitions, but he had a wife and child and another was on the way. Instead, he worked as a maintenance man in a factory, joined a union and eventually became a Labour party agent.

What was wrong with Britain?, he echoed through a cloud of tobacco smoke. When he was a boy, he shared with others a sense of commitment. Jerusalem was up on the hill. We knew we would never get there in our lifetime, he said, but if you went up the brae a bit you could just see it – enough to keep the faith. But not now. It was out of sight, hidden by artificial barriers erected by Labour as well as Tory governments. First it was the balance of payments. Jenkins got it right after three years, and then we lost the election. Now it was inflation. Britain had lost its sense of direction. It seemed that nobody thought of Jerusalem, or wanted to make a contribution; but of course many remembered and wanted to do something but there was no real leadership. Labour was as bad as the Tories.

I asked why a party such as Labour had failed to produce good leaders in recent years, and Hayward said that the parliamentary system was all wrong. The hours they worked were exhausting, and after a while they ceased to care. Separated from the rank and file, they became too concerned about artificial barriers to progress, such as the balance of payments and incomes policies. They forgot what the movement stood for.

As with many men of his generation, Hayward remembered the war with nostalgia. People then had a sense of companionship because of the common danger. They helped each other, and believed that this sense of companionship would be carried into civilian life. The first post-war Labour government was terrific; it achieved more than any government could wish, but people got fed up because they were always offered jam tomorrow and not today. No wonder ordinary working people got impatient. There was nothing much wrong with them, except for the feeling of being let down. And the party had let them down. They were better off than before the war, but they knew that workers in West Germany were doing much better. There was also more shift work, and many jobs were dirty, noisy and monotonous. They welcomed strikes. He knew because he had organized them, but free collective bargaining worked only for the strong.

He brooded over the winter of discontent of 1978 '79, and first said that he could not blame the lorry drivers. They had a tough job. Some of the long-distance drivers rarely saw their families; they went off on Monday morning and did not return before Saturday. Driving a big articulated in bad weather on the M1 was exhausting, but they should think of the low-paid and the weak.

Hayward saw himself as the conscience of the party, and he was obviously an old-fashioned Labour man. Had his forebears gone to the United States with the old Chartist leaders he would almost certainly have become a populist. I shall return to that powerful if misunderstood strain in the collective character of the Labour party and trade union movement later, but that afternoon Hayward reminded me of Kipling's Saxon peasant. Despite the owlish glasses, I thought that he was representative of the older generation of Labour voters who believed that they knew the difference between right and wrong, fair and unfair. Perhaps because of that old instinct he did not fully explain how the party had lost its way.

In theory at least, Labour is one of the most democratic political parties in the world, certainly more democratic than the Conservative party. Its roots reach not only back to the New Model Army, Levellers, Diggers and Chartists, but also down to the party faithful in the constituencies. Unlike the Tories, whose constituency parties are required only to provide support and get out the vote during the election campaigns for the parliamentary party, historically the Parliamentary Labour party (PLP) is supposed to be nurtured, shaped and directed by party workers and the trade unions which created the party, or the Labour Representation Committee as it was known in 1900.

In its early days, the party was not committed to the conception of the class struggle or to any coherent socialist philosophy or programme. It did not even see itself as a political party, but as a trade union and social reform movement attempting to improve the lot of the working classes. As the 1902 conference report said: Menaced on every hand in workshop, court of law, and press, trade unionism has no refuge except the ballot box and Labour representation. When the decision was taken in the following year to create the Labour party, conference insisted that its Members of Parliament should resign if they were unwilling to abide by the decisions of conference. Attlee wrote as late as 1937 that the Labour party conference laid down the policy of the Party and issued instructions which must be carried out by the executive, the affiliated organizations and its representatives in Parliament and on local authorities. The annual conference was the Parliament of the movement.*

This offended the principle laid down by Burke in his address to the electors of Bristol and the hallowed supremacy of Parliament, but arguably there was nothing wrong with that. Neither Burke nor Bagehot had concerned themselves with the working-class

* *British Political Parties*, R.T. McKenzie, Heinemann, London 1955

folk of the country. Disraeli wrote about two nations, but there was no reason why the second nation, the people, should accept the comfortable conventions of the first nation, the privileged. Their traditions were just as honourable as those inherited by iron-masters and millowners. In my Cromwellian moments, I am inclined to argue that they were more honourable, and more British.

The PLP in fact soon began to resemble the Conservative and Liberal parties, and the transformation was almost complete in 1924 when it first took office, despite the obeisances afterwards made by Attlee to the party outside Parliament. For many years the constituency parties of Labour were as deferential as their Tory opposite numbers, and the trade unions were quiescent, but the transformation to conventional politics was never completed. Left-wing activists in and outside the PLP took advantage of the party's constitution to push their own extremist and minority views. In the PLP, Marxists or the Marxist-inspired began to replace many of the older generation of non-ideological Members; and in some constituencies activists belonging or owing allegiance to a variety of angry minority parties had no difficulty in seizing control. The Left have dominated the National Executive Committee in recent years, and are largely responsible for policies which do not enjoy the support of the majority of Labour voters.

The evidence became clear in election results and public opinion polls. For instance, Labour won two general elections in 1974, but its share of the total poll was less than at any time since 1935. A few weeks before the 1979 election, *The Observer* published a RSL survey which showed that a majority of Labour voters supported the Tory proposals to ban secondary picketing, reduce the number of civil servants, lower the amount in income tax paid by the better-off and to sell council houses to tenants. In other words, they opposed the policy of their own party on four vital issues. Another survey established that a majority of Labour voters no longer favoured nationalization or increased spending on social services. Of those polled, less than one in three wanted to retain close ties between the party and the trade unions, and fewer had any sympathy for strikers.

Anthony King, Professor of Government at Essex University, observed that the organized party outside Parliament consistently chose as its leaders men who commanded little respect among the general public. In elections for the National Executive, men such as Tony Benn and Michael Foot were invariably put at or near the top of the poll although survey after survey showed that they vied with Ian Paisley as the most disliked and distrusted figures in British public life. Another survey showed that only three percent

of voters named Benn as the political leader most nearly representing their own political views, compared with 29 percent for James
Callaghan and 28 percent for Margaret Thatcher.

*

Tony Benn was still Minister for Energy when we met in his office
on Millbank just before the 1979 election. He was his usual court-
eous self, sharpening a pencil for me and offering tea although it
was soon after lunch. He sucked a small pipe and sipped tea from a
large mug. Prior to our meeting he had sent me a copy of a speech
on democratic socialism, which I had read with close attention to
find out how he would make Britain prosperous and egalitarian. It
told me more of the past, at least Benn's version of the past, than of
the future.

Britain was going down the drain because of fundamental conflicts of interest between *laissez faire* economics, industrial monopolies, free trade unions and universal adult suffrage, and they
could not be reconciled without major changes in the structure of
the economy. The conflicts were evident in the thirties when the
National government's monetarist policies led to ruthless cuts in
public spending and the dole, but failed to cure unemployment. In
the United States, the New Deal funded public works and job-
creation schemes by deficit financing, but only the impending war
with its huge rearmament programmes brought back full employment and created the wealth to pay for it. Today's challenge was to
get back to full employment without rearmament and war.

Benn reviewed three possible remedies; monetarism, corporatism and democratic socialism, and quickly dismissed the first
two. The argument for monetarism was simple and straightforward: to lift the heavy burden of taxation from industry and com-
merce, by sharply cutting public investment and expenditure, in
the hope that financial incentives would work once more and
market forces would revert to the magical role of allocating and re-
allocating resources to optimize their use. Dr. Milton Friedman,
the prophet of monetarism, had won over many bankers, indu-
strialists, economists and administrators with the beautiful simplicity of his approach. There was, however, no evidence to
suggest that monetarism would reduce the power of trade union
bargaining, or that the electorate would deliberately vote for defla-
tion and a wider gap between rich and poor.

Corporatism was the consensus view of the old British Establishment, Labour and Conservative, which for reasons of prudence rather than personal preference believed it was the best
recipe for survival. It recoiled from the social disruption mone-

tarism could bring, and called for a disciplined society where the men at the top in government, industry, banking and unions would work out a common approach and impose it by law upon their constituencies. In that modern corporatism greatly resembled feudalism it was a tested and tried system. The state and the economy would be run by a new generation of barons from modern castles in the office blocks of London and Brussels. Corporatism could last longer than the jungle economics of the monotarists, but in the long run was incompatible with a free society and in failure could be transformed into a dictatorship.

Democratic socialism was the British way of resolving those conflicts, a socialism which had grown out of our experience and was not handed down from above or received from outside. Its roots were deep in our history and had been nourished by the Bible. The British Labour movement was born out of dissenters' chapels and the struggles of factory workers for trade union rights, the parliamentary vote, a separate Labour party, and finally an explicitly socialist approach based upon a full commitment to a democratic system and personal freedom. The self-discipline of full democratic control, and not the discipline of the market place or of top people, was the best hope for the future.

The Labour party had worked on the basis that the investment gap must be filled by public investment, with proper accountability and public ownership, and that only public expenditure could convert human needs into economic demands able to command resources and help restore full employment. 'To avoid corporatism creeping in as a by-product of these public initiatives we have been working for a wider and deeper accountability of power through greater democratic control by Parliament of government and of finance and industry and of the institutions of the Labour movement itself. Parliament and MPs freely elected are the greatest safeguards for our freedom. This is clearly understood by the Labour party and Labour MPs.'

The last claim would have been dismissed by many Labour Members as a typical example of misleading Bennery. What he chose to describe as corporatism, and I as the soggy centre, was in fact the policy of the PLP; and for that matter of Len Murray, the general secretary of the Trades Union Congress, who preferred to describe it as tripartitism. Benn's description of democratic socialism was also misleading to the extent that too much was left unsaid. In subsequent discussion, which reminded me of a tutorial with Benn playing the part of a helpful don, he said that Britain could have made a go of it in 1945. We had emerged from the war with a national consensus, and indeed a great deal was achieved. He referred to the railways and energy as examples. We could have restructured the economy with intelligent investment, but profits were not reinvested and as a consequence traditional industries such as shipbuilding collapsed.

He brushed aside my suggestion that the unions might have been partly to blame because of demarcation disputes and their general reluctance to accept new technologies. The consensus, he continued, had been eroded by the sixties when Britain went through a strange period. The managers were expected to run our society. It was a widespread phenomenon; Kennedy in the United States and Pompidou in France as well as Wilson and Heath in Britain threw experience into the dustbin and assumed that politics was only a matter of fine tuning the economy. Attlee, Macmillan, Adenauer and the Chinese leaders knew differently, but they were wise men.

Experience proved that little could be achieved by tinkering with the economy. The fundamental conflict of interests had to be resolved; this was what politics was all about. Margaret Thatcher was trying to form a new consensus based on union-bashing and less public spending. Unlike Heath, who believed in a society with corporate central discipline, the Thatcher argument was intellectually respectable but it would not work. Only democratic socialism would succeed.

People did not realize that Britain was again in the lead, this time as the pioneer in government by consent. It was not a matter of ideology, but a radical reform against centralized power. The Prime Minister was more powerful than the American President, and had far more patronage. Power was still being concentrated in the Labour party, the unions, industry and publishing. These small elites were completely out of touch. Thatcher could crusade against this centralization of power, but he wanted human and not market forces to shape society. Britain could not be a just and contented society unless ordinary people had the power to reflect their own values in decisions which affected their lives. It was not a revolutionary idea, but the suggestion of democracy panicked people at the top. They did not realize that in practice democracy was conservative because there was no discipline more rigorous than your fellow men.

I could not but warm to Benn's apparent idealism, but there were too many holes in his argument. The trade unions surely had to share some of the blame for our poor economic performance. Large-scale investment was useless if they were unprepared to accept the new technologies and manning levels involved. The essential weakness of course was that the proposals which were intended to diffuse power and improve accountability could inevitably lead to more centralization. Certainly the Callaghans,

63

Healeys and Owens did not trust him, and some were convinced that his call for more democracy was a plot to deliver the party and country into the hands of undemocratic forces. Or to put it another way, his idea of democracy was uncomfortably close to that of the socalled people's democracies of the communist world.

Another cause of the distrust was personal. Like Enoch Powell and Keith Joseph, the Tory ideologue, Benn was a zealot and it could show in his eyes. Zealotry can be dangerous, and his critics also charged him with inconsistency and opportunism. For instance, he began as a supporter of British membership of the European Economic Community and then became one of its most effective critics. He had proposed that the issue should be decided by referendum in the belief that the majority of voters were against entry, and refused to accept the verdict of the electorate when it voted by two to one in favour of membership.

So much for his populism, but he continued to behave as if he had not been educated at Westminster and Oxford. His transformation from wealthy peer to man of the people was marked by the constant re-editing of his entry in *Who's Who*, from thirtyeight lines until it finally disappeared.

Perhaps only good for a giggle, although I was reminded of Orwell's Ministry of Truth. But as Patrick Cosgrove remarked in a review, for all the talk about open government, equality in a socialist society, and the cutting down of the rich to serve the poor, he and his wife were morbidly secretive about the network of family trusts that, whatever happened in Britain, would preserve American wealth for their children. With others, I found this offensive because apparently what was good enough for my goslings was not good enough for his.

He was known as Chairman Benn, Citizen Benn and Ayatollah Benn, but there was small reason to believe that he would emerge as the leader should the extreme left wing ever take over the party. Or if he did, he would not survive for long. The fact remained that at the time of writing there was no conceivable future Labour government in which he would not hold office.

*

The Labour party is similar in many ways to the Democratic party of the United States. Both can claim to represent the working class majority. Both attract intellectuals, academics and middle-class men and women with social consciences who in the past at least provided ideas and much of the leadership. The Democrats once had the Solid South, but this had crumbled since the civil rights policy of the party won over the black vote from the Republicans.

Labour is now also attracting the immigrant vote. Both parties are to that extent people's parties in that they try to do good for the greatest number.

Both parties also suffer from acute internal divisions and rivalries. The Democrats are often portrayed in the American press as tearing themselves apart, but there the similarities end. Unlike the TUC, the AFL-CIO is not an integral part of the Democratic party. Nor does it have formal representation on the national committee or at the conventions. The Democrats do not have a highly-centralized organization; indeed, the Democratic National Committee has little power because of the federal nature of the party. Each state has its own party and manages its own affairs, including the selection of candidates for state and national office. They are often more concerned with winning local elections than electing a Democratic President and congressional majorities in Washington. Moreover, the Democratic leaderships in the Senate and House of Representatives cannot assume the loyalty of the men and women they are supposed to lead, as in turn a Democratic President cannot assume their loyalty and support.

Other differences are less tangible but more important. The Democrats have their left and right, but they are not ideologically divided as are Labour's left and right. Democrats with union badges on their coveralls rarely question the capitalist system, and very few of the intellectuals question the United States Constitution. For all their differences, and periodic suicidal bouts, Democrats accept the system. They want to improve, not change it. Their loyalty to country can be embarrassing for Britons living among them, but generally it is not jingoism. They believe, even after the terrible traumas of the sixties and seventies, that great good can be achieved in the land of the free and the home of the brave without changing its institutions. It is this simple belief that unites them.

The Labour left and right are seldom united, except when they sing Auld Lang Syne at the end of another self-destructive annual conference. They are divided by a gulf which cannot be bridged by simple loyalty to country and belief in its institutions. The vast proportion of Labour supporters are on the right, and accept the established order. Allowing for national differences, their loyalty to country is not so very different from that of Democrats. On the left, however, the revolutionary zeal will never be quenched by improving the national well-being. They will never be satisfied by doing good for the greatest number. Their concept of social justice and equality cannot be realized without destroying the country's constitutional system.

I am not suggesting that the entire left wing is disloyal in the

65

accepted sense of the word. Willy Hamilton, Member for Fife, Central, is against the Monarchy but there is a larger loyalty to country in which arguably the Queen is only a convenient constitutional cypher. It remains that many of them are motivated by a curious international loyalty which requires them to attack British institutions but remain silent when crimes against humanity committed by socialist countries cry out for universal condemnation. They believe that their ill-defined notions of social justice and equality can only be achieved with the kind of state apparatus found in the Soviet Union and eastern Europe. They argue that the British version of, say, East Germany and Czechoslovakia will be different – Britain has always been different – but if they succeed the Labour party will have betrayed the working class of this country which it is supposed to represent.

This is the awful division within the Labour party, but that said the right wing, moderates, social democrats – call them what you will – did not always act intelligently when they were in complete control. Clement Attlee achieved a remarkable unity within the party with the help of Bevin and the then complaisant trade union leadership, in part because members who also belonged to the Communist party and other then proscribed political organizations, were expelled. With that kind of party unity Attlee maintained a degree of national unity which no Prime Minister, Tory or Labour, can now hope to achieve. For instance, he used troops to break strikes damaging to the national interest. More important, he presided over the greatest social revolution in British history. Given the much-vaunted English love of self-effacement and under statement, Attlee should be a greater folk hero than Churchill, but as already noted he and Bevin decided that Britain would be a nuclear power and also ordered a massive conventional rearmament programme.

Lord Croham, the former Douglas Allen and one of Britain's most powerful civil servants, argued years later that this was the first major strategic mistake of the postwar period. He said over lunch at the Bank of England one day that at the time Britain was sorting itself out economically and approaching the point of postwar economic takeoff. We could have kept abreast if not in front of the West German *Wirtschaftswunder* but for that massive mis-allocation of manpower and resources to rearmament which first put us on the slippery slope to national decline.

The left opposed rearmament, Nato membership and the special relationship with the United States, although not necessarily for the reasons given by Croham. Most of them were clamorously anti-American and silently pro-Soviet but the Keep Left movement acquired legitimacy in 1951 when Aneurin Bevan, a great working-class leader, resigned from office because of differences with Cabinet colleagues over defence and social services expenditure.

Bevan became the leader of the party's dissident left, but at the party conference six years later he helped to defeat a composite resolution demanding unilateral nuclear disarmament. He made up his differences with the party leader, Hugh Gaitskell, and became deputy leader of the Opposition. Gaitskell was a decent man, but arguably Bevan should have been the party leader. He had his flaws, but within the party his working-class background gave him a natural authority which Gaitskell, the former Oxford don, could not hope to achieve. He could have won over the non-Marxist left, and the magic of his rhetoric would also have helped to unite the party and set it on a new course. It was not to be. Bevan tragically died in 1960, the year when the Campaign for Nuclear Disarmament eventually won over enough delegates to persuade the annual conference to vote for unilateral disarmament. Its victory was short-lived, but Gaitskell also died. When the party was returned to power in 1964 the new Prime Minister, Harold Wilson, went to Washington and reconfirmed Britain's role as a nuclear power and junior partner in the Anglo-American alliance.

I was then Washington correspondent of *The Times*, and could hardly believe my ears. There was first the personal sense of shame – which was of no consequence of course – of having to report a Prime Minister who out-acted Danny Kaye as Walter Mitty; and more important, the sad realization that eight years after Suez Labour had produced a leader who still hankered after imperial responsibility and grandeur. I can remember him briefing British correspondents at the embassy, and claiming that apart from the United States we were the only western country which was a world power. We had to do our bit, and his eyes misted over as he spoke of the Royal Navy keeping the peace east of Suez.

Labour was apparently incapable of arriving at an honourable and realistic position supportable by a country of the second rank. It seemed that the only two choices for the party were either unilateral nuclear disarmament, which actually meant neutrality and possibly eventual subservience to the Soviet Union, or world-power status with its crushing economic burden.

Wilson's posturing was all the more surprising because he had resigned from office with Bevan back in 1951. He was a shrewd politician, but apart from that romantic streak he also accepted Anthony Crosland's argument that the expanding world economy would allow Labour to achieve its objectives without facing up to painful reality. The argument was philosophically false; economic expansion was no more infinite than the supply of fossil fuels, and it began to falter before Arab producers and then OPEC began to increase the price of oil.

The failures of the moderates thus opened the way for the left, and at a time when the party was changing. The decisive shift came from within the trade union movement. Frank Cousins of the Transport and General was the first to flex his muscles by calling damaging strikes and trying to use CND as a weapon to destroy Gaitskell. Others followed. They were the new generation of union leaders, and were more political than their predecessors. They and their members had also grown accustomed to regular wage increases during the Macmillan period of relative prosperity and low unemployment, and after Labour's return to power in 1964 reacted angrily to Wilson's efforts to prop up the pound and his proposed trade union legislation.

There was another shift within the party. Young activists, the first generation of working-class graduates, were not interested in status symbols such as nuclear weapons. The special relationship was hateful because it moved Wilson to support what they saw as American imperialism in Vietnam and elsewhere. They should have been natural recruits for Labour, but many joined Trotskyist splinter groups and practised entryism. This was the label for the strategy devised by the Fourth International to take over the Labour party. One Trot, as they came to be known, tried to penetrate Transport House by courting the daughter of a high official but his dastardly plot failed when he fell in love with the girl and became a good social democrat. Others were more successful in infiltrating the Young Socialists and capturing many constituency parties.

This was not difficult because of the decline in party membership. The official total of about 600,000 was complete invention, made possible by the party rule that each constituency party must pay a minimum affiliation fee for 1,000 members, but the true figure was less than half. In some safe Labour seats there were so few members, that the local party was easily captured by the entryists. They were still entering the party and the unions when the 1970 election was lost, and the left, which was always more effective in opposition, was ready to seize the opportunity.

The story is well told by Michael Hatfield, a member of *The Times* political staff, in his book *The House the Left Built*.* The left held a disproportionately large number of seats on the NEC, but still a minority. They could have been frustrated from the beginning, but the moderates were not prepared to devote enough time to committee work. Wilson was busy writing his memoirs, and his lack of interest was inexcusable. The NEC is not the supreme body

* Gollancz, London 1978

68

within the party, despite the theory, but the left recognized its latent power and knew how to use it.

Their aim was to redirect the party towards their socialist objectives, and they succeeded in producing the most radical party programme in thirty years. It included an economic and industrial policy which committed the next Labour government, much to the dismay of most members of the Shadow Cabinet and the party's well-wishers, to an unprecedented extension of state intervention.

The battlefield was once again the ambiguous commitment in Clause Four of the party's constitution to 'secure for the workers by hand or by brain the full fruits of their industry and the most equitable distribution thereof that may be possible, upon the basis of the common ownership of the means of production, distribution and exchange, and the best obtainable system of popular administration and control of each industry or service'. This nationalization clause was one of the concessions made to the left for supporting the constitution when it was drafted in 1918. Little importance was attached to it at the time, but over the years it had divided the party between the left and the moderates.

Not that the latter, or the Conservatives for that matter, were opposed to nationalization as a means of rationalizing industry or rescuing inefficient and bankrupt enterprises. The Tories nationalized the electricity grid system, established a public monopoly in civil aviation and brought London Transport under public control before the second world war. The Attlee government nationalized the railways, internal airways, road transport, gas, electricity, coal, iron and steel for much the same reasons, and then lost its enthusiasm for public ownership. Gaitskell and Crosland moved the party away from its socialist founding faith towards social reform and egalitarianism. The moderate majority was won over to the concept of public control of the economy by Keynesian fiscal and monetary measures, but for the Marxist-influenced left nationalization remained an article of faith. Without it they could not hope to establish socialism in Britain.

The draft programme produced by the NEC in 1973 went a long way towards achieving that objective. It was seen by the more radical only as a first step, but the estimated financial cost was astronomical. The social policies alone would have soaked up all available resources, and the total commitments would have cost £5,500 million a year at 1973 prices. The main proposal was the establishment of the National Enterprise Board. There was nothing particularly socialist about this proposal, similar bodies had operated effectively in Italy and elsewhere; but the NEB was to acquire twenty-five of the country's largest manufacturing companies. They were to be nationalized without compensation, a policy which Callaghan later described as legalized robbery. Another 100 large companies were to be required to sign planning agreements, which in effect would have established government control of manufacturing.

A new Industry Bill was to be drafted to provide the next Labour government with all the powers needed to meet its socialist objectives, and there was much more. It amounted to almost total centralized planning and direction. The economic future of the country would be firmly in the hands of politicians and bureaucrats. Only wages escaped, presumably as a temporary sop to the unions, although it was difficult to see how a planned society could work even with the degree of inefficiency achieved in the Soviet Union if such a large item was left to free collective bargaining.

Wilson threatened to veto the programme, and the scene was set for one of those furious debates in which soul-searching Labour politicians love to indulge to the despair of the average Labour voter. Benn defended the programme of course, and even John Kenneth Galbraith, the Harvard professor, joined in. He welcomed the programme as an improvement on the trivial discussion at universities, for which everyone should be grateful however damaging its effect upon Labour's electoral chances.

Crosland said that the programme risked deceiving the public by suggesting that nationalization automatically furthered the basic socialist aims of equality, justice and democracy. The party could not justify a blanket threat to every large firm in Britain based on the misleading assumption that a change of ownership would of itself produce miraculous results. Edmund Dell condemned the NEB as a monster. It would be by far the largest industrial enterprise in Europe and probably the world, a dinosaur which no Minister for Trade and Industry could control.

Whether or not this promise or threat of socialism was responsible, in 1974 Labour returned to power with only a majority of three. It could hardly be said to have a mandate for such radical change, but Benn told the Young Socialists that as Minister for Industry he was preparing to implement the strategy set out in the programme. The National Enterprise Board was indeed established, although with greatly reduced powers, but much else of the left-inspired programme was dumped when hyper-inflation almost swept the country down the drain.

*

The failure of the left to impose its programme upon the Wilson government in 1974 was seen as only a temporary setback in their inexorable progress towards socialism. They were convinced that history was on their side, and that public ownership and protectionism would solve the country's economic problems. It mattered not that their prescription of protectionism could not protect a trading country such as Britain unless it adopted a siege economy and accepted lower living standards and less personal freedom on the eastern European model. Presumably some of them were not averse to that, despite all the available evidence that the majority of the electorate in Britain, as elsewhere in the EEC, preferred the social democratic approach.

They continued to press their own solution, whatever the majority wanted, and the party's constitution provided them with the opportunity. This meant, in the words of David Marquand,* the former Labour politician who had given up the struggle and sought the relative safety of a provincial university campus, that a future Labour government would again have to confront the British crisis with one hand tied behind its back. The moderates still controlled the party, but they could only remain in control by paying endless quantities of moral Danegeld to the left. It rarely amounted to much in terms of policy but it made an enormous difference to the party's style and posture. They also had to cosset the trade union establishment, which he saw as the greatest single impediment to the regeneration of British industry.

The moderates knew that the gulf between themselves and the left was the deepest in British politics, but they had to pretend that they were really on the same side of a much deeper gulf. They had to pretend that despite occasional differences of emphasis, they were all part of the same Labour movement ranged in fundamental conflict with the bosses and exploiters on the opposite side of the House of Commons; that, so far from belonging to an alien species, they were merely more circumspect members of the same species. It was humbug, but dangerous and corrupting humbug.

It meant that the party leaders could never talk honestly to their followers, to each other or to the country. It also meant, since the left were still hostile to private enterprise as such, that the party could never adopt a strategy openly and explicitly designed to make private enterprise more profitable. It finally meant that it could not adopt a strategy openly and explicitly designed to overcome the crisis because the British crisis could not be overcome without making private enterprise more profitable.

Marquand was quickly overtaken by events. Two motions passed with large majorities at the 1979 conference in Brighton

* *The Listener*, May 10, 1979

71

demonstrated that the left was now the most powerful single force at the conference as well as the most influential on the NEC and in many of the constituency parties. The first motion required the automatic re-selection of Members of Parliament between general elections, which would enable the left in the constituencies they controlled to cow moderate MPs or replace them with their own candidates.

The second gave the NEC exclusive responsibility for the party manifesto. A third motion calling for the election of the party leader by an electoral college instead of the PLP was defeated, but in effect the left had turned tables and was excluding the moderates from the party's institutions. The leadership defeat was of little consequence if the constituencies dictated policy to the Members. The independence of the PLP could be eventually eroded from within, and the power of the left would then be complete.

The victories were all the more disturbing because they could not have been won without a large union vote. While the trade unions still provided most of the moderate members of the NEC, the conference votes indicated that communists and the various Trotskyists had become more influential in some unions and therefore in the direction of the Labour party. The moderates should not have been surprised, the industrial organizer of the Communist party had held regular strategy meetings with communist trade union leaders throughout the conference; but the question was no longer when the moderates would get rid of the left but how they could hope to survive the leftist tide.

During the first heady moments after their victory at Brighton, many of the younger activists believed that the future, so often promised and postponed, would soon be theirs. They assumed that the Thatcher government's market approach to our problems would fail, that Labour would be swept back to power and that they would be in control of the party. The irreversible swing to socialism would then take place. It is possible, if unlikely. The only certainty is that the left had over the years succeeded in diminishing the effectiveness of Labour as a party of government and an engine of change. It had helped to push Britain down the slippery slope of national decline.

The moderates could not of course escape their share of responsibility, although one must be careful in apportioning blame. Men and women, including journalists such as myself, are imperfect, vain or weak. It is pointless to set impossibly high standards of personal and political behaviour to which no human can even aspire. That said, the moderates did not have to permit entryism or later to refuse to publish the Underhill report on its success. They could have spent more time in the constituencies and given more attention to the NEC. They could have ignored the left instead of moving to the left to maintain a spurious unity. The left had nowhere to go. Wilson with his constant reference to This Great Movement of Ours was the worst offender, but when with Barbara Castle he tried to introduce trade union reform in 1969, other moderate leaders gave him little support. Indeed, Callaghan made defeat certain.

The moderate leaders of the second post-war generation are now either dead, retired or approaching the end of their political careers. The rising generation, such as Roy Hattersley, David Owen, William Rodgers, Peter Shore, Eric Varley and Shirley Williams, are decent and competent men and women who could make their mark in any social democratic party if only in a modest way. They and their like are nevertheless the hope for the future if the Labour party is once again to represent its natural constituency, but they are also tarnished. They have paid Danegeld to the left, including Shirley Williams.

At one time it was easy to see why many people hoped that she would be Britain's first woman Prime Minister. An intelligent and warm-hearted person, she was often gently caricatured as a Hampstead intellectual too interested in ideas to give much thought to her appearance, although when we met she was neatly dressed in a woollen suit with a single row of dark coral beads. Her hair had been recently set, and she looked like everybody's favourite aunt – albeit an aunt with a political science degree and ministerial experience.

The main trouble with Britain, she said, was that the class system still cast a heavy shadow over the land, although her constituency, Hertford and Stevenage, was different. The majority was skilled or semi-skilled workers and classless in the American way. They had homes of their own and cars, and wanted to do well by their children. I suggested that this was a fair description not only of people living in new towns such as Stevenage but of at least half of the population, and many others had similar aspirations. They were sons and daughters of working-class parents who had been liberated from the old class attitudes. Perhaps the majority belonged to trade unions, but at home they lived a passing semblance of the good bourgeois life, and liked it. To that extent the old class system no longer cast a long shadow, except in blighted industrial areas and inner cities.

Williams appeared to be the ideal candidate for such a constituency, but she lost her seat in the 1979 election in a swing greater than the national swing against Labour. Her defeat was inexplicable except that she had paid too much Danegeld to the left. She had even appeared on the Grunwick picket line along with members of the Tribune group, Trots and union heavies such as Arthur Scargill. Married couples hoping that their children would grow up in a prosperous and orderly society could not have enjoyed television shots of their Member siding with thugs roughing up the police.

The Observer afterwards published an article asking which side she was really on. It was a good question in that it posed the dilemma Labour moderates had created for themselves and the country.

FIVE

United We Stand

Peregrine Worsthorne of *The Sunday Telegraph* is a Tory by nature and (I almost wrote but) a very good journalist. I have always read him with pleasure, and often profited from his observations. Such was the case during the 1979 election campaign when by a stroke of good fortune his car broke down in the middle of Spaghetti Junction. Why good fortune? Because the experience taught him more about the roots of trade union and Labour party loyalty than listening to any amount of socialist platform rhetoric.

He wrote that middle-class people were seldom made to feel helpless, impotent or totally dependent on forces they could not understand or control. For them, the world did not usually look impersonally menacing because their lives were cushioned by a thick protective texture of family and social relationships and connexions. There was always somebody in the know to turn to, a way round every difficulty, a door waiting to be pushed open. Life might not be easy, but was seldom implacable, cold or, above all, impersonal. For such people, standing on your own feet was not really quite what it sounds.

But standing on his two feet beside a broken-down car in the middle of a motorway maze, Worsthorne felt utterly lost, abandoned and longing for Big Brother to come to the rescue. It was an alien universe offering no point of human contact; man without a machine was simply out of place – a mere cypher.

For many working people, Worsthorne continued, that was how they felt for much, if not all, of their lives. How could a worker in British Leyland be expected to feel captain of his fate? Poverty was no longer a problem, technology had produced enough goods to go round, but it had also produced patterns of work (the computerized factory), patterns of living (the tower block) and patterns of recreation (television) which reduced men's individuality, forcing them to huddle together in search of some kind of collective strength. They looked to trade unions and socialism to give them new forms of protection.

Worsthorne went on to suggest that ordinary people were becoming disillusioned with the Labour party as earlier for much the same reason they had become disillusioned with the Tory party: it had failed to produce a society in which they felt at home. He was probably more than half right, but most working people still sought the protection of unions. Admittedly some were also becoming disillusioned; brutal strikes were no part of a society in which they felt at home, but their unions still offered them the best protection in this Spaghetti Junction world.

This simple and indisputable fact must be understood before questioning the power of trade unions, as anybody who grew up poor must know. On one of the plate-glass windows of my mother's coffee shop in London's East End was the legend 'United we stand, Divided we fall'. For me, it was the First Commandment, offering the only way out of the poverty of a then Tory-misgoverned country. Not that it helped casual dockworkers in those days, but within thirty years the unions had become a power in the land, the dominant power according to some. Certainly their victories over the Wilson government in 1969 and the Heath and Callaghan governments which followed gave them a sense of power which they were to use without compunction or compassion.

That was not the end of it. I can remember meeting Michael Foot on Hampstead Heath soon after he became Secretary of State for Employment in 1974. We were accustomed to walking our dogs together, and our previous conversations had more often than not been bantering in tone. I could never understand why this great parliamentarian and libertarian should puruse leftist policies which could only lead to the curbing of our liberties. It was also surprising that the nonconformist conscience of the House had accepted a ministerial appointment because I had always assumed that he saw his first duty as attacking authority and not joining it. That Sunday morning he was suitably ministerial, and said that after the three-day work week his first task was to get the country back to work. He was apparently convinced that the promises of the Labour manifesto, which included the repeal of the Industrial Relations Act, would ensure the full cooperation of the unions. I was not, but wished him and all of us well.

The Trades Union Congress had in fact dictated much of the industrial relations policy of the new Labour government, which had committed itself to the principles of the so-called social contract. This was another considerable victory; never before had the TUC moved so close to the centre of national power, but they did not feel morally bound by the contract to support the government's efforts to control the worst inflation and balance-of-payments deficit in our history. Or perhaps closer to the truth, after defeating Labour and Tory attempts to bring industrial relations within the law the TUC could not control its affiliated unions. The members of the TUC's General Council, who were deferentially treated like statesmen because they were assumed to represent organized labour, were as powerless as the government.

They must have known. The TUC had very little direct authority within the movement, and over the years power within the affiliated unions had been moving steadily from the general secretaries to shop stewards. There was something to be said for this transfer of power. Because of their slow organic growth, many British trade unions were genuinely democratic in structure if not in practice. General secretaries had rarely been given the authority of American union presidents. Given their democratic structure, the fact that most British unions had relatively few paid officials, and the smallness of many concerns they had organized, it was natural that shop stewards should have some authority to treat with their employers. Arguably it was more efficient in that disputes could be avoided if dissatisfaction on the shop floor was dealt with at any early stage; and certainly the system worked well for many years.

It still worked reasonably well in some areas and industries, many of which had not had a strike for as long as most people could remember, but elsewhere shop stewards had increasingly become the cause of much of the industrial strife which had blighted British industry for years. There were a number of obvious reasons for this, but clearly the TUC was in no position to guarantee the industrial peace Foot and other members of the Wilson government thought they had been promised.

The General Council must also have known of the growing militancy inside many unions. In 1972, for instance, Arthur Scargill, the Yorkshire miners' leader, helped to organize flying pickets which overwhelmed the police at the Saltley coking dump. Without being overly dramatic, they defeated the forces of law and order and the government knuckled under. In the same year five shop stewards at the Midland Cold Storage Company were imprisoned for illegal blacking, and a general strike was avoided only after the Official Solicitor asked the Industrial Relations Court to review their case. One function of the Official Solicitor is to see that justice is done to those undefended in court, but clearly the so-called Pentonville Five were released because the government was afraid of what might well be described as an insurrection. Again this may sound dramatic, but the fact of the matter was that the government submitted to the threat of brute force. It was no less insurrectionary than if the unions had stormed the gates of Buckingham Palace.

Nevertheless, two years later the TUC demanded its Danegeld

77

from the new Labour government. Apart from the repeal of the Industrial Relations Act, the statutory incomes policy and the National Industrial Relations Court were abolished. Legislation increasing union immunities and giving more employment protection to workers was enacted. Food subsidies and tighter price controls were introduced, rents frozen and pensions increased. The Advisory, Conciliation and Arbitration Service was created, and the redistribution of incomes as well as industrial democracy was promised. To quote Eric Wigham*, by the end of 1974 the trade unions' demands for power had reached a new dimension. They had defeated two governments and had now got one largely subservient to their wishes. They were claiming to share with the employers the controls of industry and to share with the government the control of the national economy.

This was their Danegeld, but the TUC was not in charge of the marauding longboats. The strikes continued, despite the reassuring platitudes of the leaders and the subservience of the Wilson government. Excluding the miners' strike, more than nine million working days were lost that year, some two million more than in 1973. The presses were worked overtime to print money to meet the surge of inflation largely generated by the 28.5 percent rise in weekly wage rates during the year. The country was going down the drain again, and the final stage of decline was averted only by another incomes policy and the disciplines imposed by the International Monetary Fund in return for its massive support.

Disaster was avoided, the inflation rate was briefly brought down to single figures, but little or nothing was learned. The TUC still in effect demanded power without responsibility, and during the last winter of Labour's administration affiliated unions went marauding again after three years of wage restraint. The secondary picketing of striking lorry drivers further damaged industry. The dead went unburied, and hospital ancillary workers announced that they were prepared to see patients die in order that they could screw a few more pounds a week extra from the hospital authorities. (It is interesting that in this welfare state union leaders always refer to the hospital and local authorities as the employers.)

Such acts of union inhumanity no doubt helped the Conservative party to win the 1979 election, but this political price only angered some militants. A delegate to the annual conference of the National Union of Public Employees demanded industrial action if the Labour policy of phasing out pay beds in hospitals was reversed. He said that private patients were 'rich bastards deserving to be denied hospital care'. This was an extraordinary

* *Strikes and the Government 1893–1974*. Macmillan, 1976

extension of class hatred, but the delegate was not reprimanded. He was afterwards dismissed for painting the slogan 'NUPE rules' on a hospital wall, and his workmates called for a one-day strike.

Militants were not alone responsible for inhumane acts. Men who objected to the closed shop, or sinned against the union rule book, were expelled and rendered unemployable in their own trades. Rather like earlier unfortunates who were dispossessed by the Enclosures, they were victims of a cruel system.

This was not the new world in which ordinary people could feel at home. It could be a menacing world, making them feel as helpless, impotent or totally dependent on forces they could not control as in the bad old days before unions became powerful. Nevertheless, the majority remained loyal to their unions; few of them were prepared to speak out to protect a workmate or oppose an unnecessary strike, or, for that matter, attend union meetings and use their democratic rights to achieve a better world. It seemed that with their individuality reduced, the majority accepted union protection as peasants once accepted the protection of their feudal lord. Whether the lord combined against the king or fought for him in a civil or foreign war was none of their business. They remained loyal because otherwise they could lose his protection and their livelihoods.

*

Such ugly incidents were not the invention of the Tory press as some union leaders claimed, nor were they typical of the movement. More than eleven million men and women belonged to unions affiliated to the TUC and only a few were mean and nasty. The vast majority were decent working folk. It takes all sorts to make a world, as my old mother used to say, and indeed to make a union. That said, the movement had attracted more than its fair share of militants, communists and Trotskyists.

They included the socalled entryists, referred to in the last chapter, who emerged from the universities and polytechnics in the sixties and seventies. To some extent history was repeating itself in that they were not so very different from Burgess, Maclean, Philby, Blunt and others who earlier worked for the Russians because they arrogantly believed that Britain was not a fit place for them to grow up in. The Trots had made some progress in the white-collar and public service unions, and were responsible for most of the nastier incidents in the winter of discontent. The communists, probably because they were better disciplined, were more effective. Some of the mineworkers' leaders who helped bring down the Heath government belonged or had belonged to the party, and the leader of the Pentonville Five was a party member. They were also strong in the car and building industries, and throughout British industry had fixed or influenced union elections because of the apathy of the rank and file.

Nevertheless, it would be wrong to assume that they were wholly responsible for industrial unrest and general bloody-mindedness. The main reason was the refusal of the trade union leadership to accept any restraint on their power. Their rejection of one of the essential disciplines of any civilized society perforce led to confrontation with the government, indiscipline on the shop floor, poor production and, above all, disequilibrium in British society.

Not that Len Murray saw it that way when we met in Congress House. The General Secretary of the TUC was a thoroughly decent man, and had probably suffered more in recent years than chairmen of strike-bound companies. His sad face suggested an infinite capacity for absorbing pain, and stress and overwork had led to two heart attacks. It was also a friendly and intelligent face. A Shropshire lad, and son of a farm worker, Murray won a scholarship to the local grammar school and after war service read economics at New College, Oxford. He joined the economics department of the TUC in 1947, and moved steadily up the ladder until he was appointed General Secretary in 1973.

The British disease, he said over a bottle of German wine, was old age, old institutions, old industrial assets and old attitudes. You could say it was maturity, but there was only a thin line between maturity and senility. The trade union movement was a reflection of British society, a mirror image of its qualities and defects. It reflected the uncertainty of our society. His dilemma was that he genuinely did not know if the British wanted a quiet life or the good life they saw on their television screens, and they could not have both. At the 1978 TUC conference, delegates had demanded higher wages and a 35-hour week although they ought to have known that they could only have one or the other.

This enervating environment remained unchanged, but not for want of trying. More institutions had been created since the second world war than he had had hot dinners. We were once reluctant to learn from others, but were now more than willing. The Advisory, Conciliation and Arbitration Service had evolved from the American experience.

The TUC went to Sweden looking for an incomes policy and returned with a manpower policy. The National Economic Development Council (which Murray helped to establish) was stimulated by the French Planning Commission.

Trade unionists, and Britons generally, were resistant to change because we were a conservative society. We had become more conservative as we become more insecure. We wanted to hang on to what we have got, but there had been some change. We were a more mobile society, in 1977 nearly ten million changed jobs. The older industries such as mining and railways had been run down with union acquiescence. Lancashire had moved from textiles to engineering.

The trade union movement had also changed, from Ernest Bevin to Jack Jones. It had to change because members were now better educated and more articulate. The more intelligent wanted a piece of the action; at least he hoped so because if you wanted change you first had to change the people. Bevinism, that is a powerful centralized leadership, was no longer an alternative except in extraordinary circumstances. Power had shifted to the shop floor. The rank and file could not be expected to accept responsibility unless they were involved in making decisions. Some shop stewards did not like this because they were reluctant to share their authority, but it had to be done.

Murray admitted ruefully that this internal shift of power, and his hope of instilling responsibility among the rank and file, was a long and painful process but insisted that there was not an acceptable alternative. Legislation and a legalistic apparatus would not work even if a government tried to impose it with guns, and the Trots and the monetarists could only lead the country to anarchy. Perhaps we needed some legislation and an element of monetarism, but he had to stay within the broad central stream of trade unionism. Margaret Thatcher worried him because she could deliver the movement into the hands of extremists.

We finished the bottle as the light dimmed in the courtyard with its symbolic statue suspended against a fan of marble. Unbeknown to me, Murray's wife Heather was patiently waiting for him in the outer office. It had been another long day for him, but he seemed to be a worried man who wanted to explain his hopes and fears. The paradox about unions, he said, was that they were about individuals and the right of a man to answer back to his boss. The movement must never forget that or otherwise we would become the monster some people said we were. Lord Denning (the Master of the Rolls whose libertarianism had led him on more than one occasion to find against unions) was an admirable man, but did not understand the collective nature of our society. He was too fascinated by the nineteenth century, and did not see that the freedom of the individual could best be sustained by unions.

Murray's analysis of the causes of our national decline was disturbing because of its innate pessimism, the depth of which I

81

had not encountered during this enquiry except in the company of a few very senior civil servants. No less disturbing was his criticism of Denning, and his apparent inability to see that such judges tried to defend the freedom of the individual from the misuse of power, whether by government, employers or unions. Murray reflected the view of most members of the TUC General Council who dismissed their judgements as judicial intervention in an area which was not the concern of the courts.

They were so angered by Denning that in the last weeks of the Callaghan government the TUC sought means of making union legal immunity total. I was reminded of the American robber barons at the turn of the century who treated their workers badly and sought a similar immunity. This was well described by the historian Charles Beard*: 'If corporations cannot provide employment for the millions of the American proletariat – for such we have, in spite of all the claptrap to the contrary – can corporate persons expect to protect themselves forever, through Constitutional and judicial processes, against the distresses and distempers of natural persons twisting and turning in their search for the rights of life, liberty and property declared in the American creed?' The wheel had turned full circle, but the irony escaped British trade union leaders.

Their degree of statutory immunity from actions at law was considerable. Lord Denning† wrote, 'These statutes range from the Trade Disputes Act of 1906 to the latest Act in 1976. In between there was the Industrial Relations Act of 1971. It was ill-fated. Important parts of it were repealed. We have now a comprehensive range of statutes which grant immunity for any act done by a union or workers "in contemplation or furtherance of a trade dispute". It is not actionable for them to induce a breach of any contract – not only a contract of employment – but any contract. Nor is it actionable to interfere with its performance. Not only is it not actionable – it is also not unlawful. It is not to be regarded as the doing of an unlawful act or the use of unlawful means . . . The words "trade dispute" are defined in comprehensible words so as to cover nearly every dispute in which a trade union is likely to be engaged.'

Denning concluded that common law had done a good deal to prevent the abuse of power by a powerful group of employers or employees. It had held that the members of the group and its officers were liable if they were guilty of using unlawful means or pursuing some unlawful end. But this did not apply to trade unions. Parliament had granted them immunity. It was not for the judges to cavil at this, or criticize it. Parliament thought, and no doubt

* 'Corporations and Natural Rights', *Virginia Quarterly Review*, July 1936.
† *The Discipline of Law*, Butterworths, 1979

with reason, that the law should have nothing to do with trade disputes. They were to be solved by the good sense of the parties and not by the judges. Any intervention by the law would provoke such resentment that it would only make matters worse. Such being the philosophy of the day, it behoved these powerful bodies to act with responsibility towards society at large and not out of any sectional interest of their own. The law could do nothing, save in the very few cases when they stepped outside the pale of immunity granted by Parliament.

The fact of the matter was that many unions failed to act with responsibility towards society despite solemn and binding agreements such as the social contract and the more recent concordat. With Bevinism dead, it was incapable of replacing the discipline of law with its own internal discipline. The hopes for responsible democracy and discipline on the shop floor might not be illusory, but Murray admitted that it would be a long and painful process.

The question remained why the TUC rejected the discipline of law when its absence had helped to weaken its own authority, encouraged industrial unrest, impoverished its members and hastened the decline of the country. Part of the answer was buried in the past, when the law had hardly been impartial. (It had taken me many years to be persuaded that the law and the police were not only concerned with defending privilege.) A more recent reason was the communist background of some union leaders. Another was that even some moderate leaders saw the trade unions as a political movement, although very few of them were as outspoken as Arthur Scargill.

The President of the Yorkshire Area of the National Union of Mineworkers was a big and brash man of early middle age with more than his fair share of the animal energy of rural and industrial peasants. He was only fifteen when he went to work underground and joined the Young Communist League. He switched to the Labour party later, but remained convinced that the path to power lay through the trade union movement and not a political party. He believed that a Marxist society could only be achieved by industrial conflict involving the rank and file. In other words, the average British worker could be persuaded to man the picket lines but not the barricades. Once politicized, the unions could then capture the Labour party.

In an interview*, in which he discussed the part played by flying pickets in bringing down the Heath government, Scargill said that they did not fight a wage battle but a class war. It was them and us. He was out to defeat the Heath government, and the only way to wage the war was to attack the vulnerable points; the power sta-

* *New Left Review*, June 1975

tions, coke and coal depots and the ports. 'We wished to paralyse the nation's economy. It's as simple as that.'

He enlisted the help of student organizations at Essex University, whose dormitories, at the taxpayers' expense, were used as a staging camp for 1,000 flying pickets. 'The first thing that we did was to tell them that we were in charge . . . We had the International Marxist Group, the International Socialists, the Workers' Revolutionary Party and all the other organizations . . . agreeing with us that they would sink their differences: that we would have to fight one common enemy and that we had no time to discuss whether Trotsky said X, Y or Z in 1873.'

The powerlessness of the union's national leadership was apparent when Scargill's guerrilla tactics were compared with the union's advice on picketing. All branches had been advised that it was lawful to picket a workplace or any other place except a person's home, provided that they did no more than peacefully communicate information or peacefully persuade workers to abstain from work. It was unlawful to interfere or prevent persons or vehicles from entering premises, and to use violence. Mass picketing which caused an obstruction could be a breach of the peace. There was more, but it did not prevent Scargill from waging his class war.

Apart from his revolutionary Marxism, Scargill was typical of many other union leaders in that he saw the trade movement and not a political party as the road to political power. There were no doubt historical reasons for this. Disraeli extended the franchise but his theory of two nations survived unimpaired. The early struggle for more pay, less working hours and decent conditions was the real stuff of politics for the working class, and could then only be achieved by trade union action. London was a distant place for most miners and factory workers, and Westminster belonged to that other nation. The Labour party was of course created by the unions to extend the struggle to Westminster, but most of the natural leaders stayed within the movement and changed the face of British politics. They not only helped to bring down three governments, before the Tories were returned to power in 1979, they had succeeded in changing the direction of the country. Britain was on the way to becoming a corporate state.

*

The corporate state has been defined* as 'a state based on the theory that the political community is composed of a number of diverse economic and functional groups, from which it follows

* *The Fontana Dictionary of Modern Thought*. Fontana/Collins, 1977

that the representation of the individual citizen, or his participation in government, should be based, not on the territorial location of his home but on the functional group of which, by job or
profession, he is a member. Theoretically the corporative bodies
(corporations or estates) should be autonomous as were the
medieval "estates" and "guilds" admired by the exponents of the
theory of the corporate state.'

As far as I know the theory has never been discussed or
approved by the TUC. Murray preferred the term tripartism, and
in our discussion tentatively suggested that it could provide a
workable framework in which Britain's decline could be arrested.
One union leader who believed that the corporate state was the
answer for many of our troubles was Clive Jenkins, the general secretary of the Association of Scientific, Technical and Managerial
Staffs.

We met in his office in north London, a large room furnished
with plush red leather chairs normally seen in television serials.
The private kitchen had a large rack of wine and there was a small
rack under a side table in his office. Jenkins had a reputation for
being a *bon vivant*, which was one reason why some people disliked him. There were others. He was physically small, rather
cocky and obviously pleased with himself. His Welsh voice
reminded some of Uriah Heep, and his flair for publicity irritated
others. All this was of little consequence of course; what mattered
was that he was an outstanding member of Disraeli's second
nation who made it through the trade union movement, and his
background probably explained some of the qualities people disliked.

Jenkins had inherited the driving ambition common among
ethnic and national minorities. He was very bright, but had to quit
school when he was only fourteen because of the death of his
father, a Port Talbot railway worker. He went to night school while
working his way up in a metallurgical laboratory, and suffered
another deep disappointment when he failed to get a place at
Ruskin College. His first union, the Association of Scientific
Workers, was too small to wield any influence. He was said to have
resented the academic progress of less bright contemporaries, but
as with many ambitious youngsters born at the bottom of the social
heap, Jenkins fell back on his own resources. Denied the advancement poor boys could expect once they had earned a university
degree, Jenkins sought a second road through the trade union
movement.

The eloquence inherited from his Primitive Methodist family
helped him to become a branch secretary of the AScW before he
was 20, and a year later he became a paid official of another small

union, the Association of Supervisory Staffs, Executives and Technicians (ASSET). He also joined the Communist party, but quit because he could not accept the deadening discipline of King Street. He stood as a prospective candidate for a safe Labour seat in 1964, but was not selected because of his brief communist past. That also rankled, but probably confirmed his belief that trade unionism was the best road to power. He continued to espouse left-wing causes and, it would seem, accept much of the ideological baggage of communism.

This did not prevent him from using some of the methods of American trade unionism. In 1968 he was active in bringing about the merger of ASSET and his first union, and two years later became general secretary. The Association of Scientific, Technical and Managerial Staffs, as the merger was called, set about extending its own strength and power, as well as the trade union movement, by organizing the middle classes. It was a novel venture, and with his flair for publicity Jenkins used some novel methods. He took full-page advertisements in *The Times* and other quality newspapers, and bought a defunct airline to get a place on the employers' side of the national joint council of the air transport industry. Beginning with fewer than 30,000 members the ASTMS claimed 500,000 in 1979 and confidently expected to recruit its millionth member within a few years.

Success did not win Jenkins much popularity within the movement, and he became a member of the TUC General Council only when the strength of his union could no longer be ignored. His flamboyant life style was resented only less than his alleged poaching of members, but there was more to it than that. Some of the other council members represented dying or decaying industries. They were fighting to defend the remnants of the first industrial revolution while Jenkins represented the future of computers and micro-processors. Many of their attitudes were as fossilized as abandoned Victorian mills and factories while mentally Jenkins was already in the world of 2001.

He appeared to bridle a bit at the label of corporatism, but said that the corporate state was inevitable. His union had 500,000 members but he actually represented two million people if you included, as one should, their families. They looked to the union to take care of them, and this gave the union the right to become politically involved and to help run the country. It was unavoidable, as even Mrs. Thatcher would eventually discover.

This view was one answer to the question frequently heard during periods of industrial anarchy: who governs Britain? Jenkins' answer was the trade unions as well as the government, the Civil Service and representatives of industry. He and Barrie

Sherman, the director of research at the ASTMS, argued* that the trade union movement was the largest and most representative voluntary and democratic movement in Britain, and that the TUC was now a body of central importance and, as such, was consulted by governments. Its general policy lobbying, and that of industry, was inevitable and would undoubtedly increase. It was the badge of a collectivized society.

Right or wrong, Jenkins seemed well placed to play the part of the politician and trade union leader. The ASTMS was well organized with efficient internal lines of communication and good research facilities. Power had moved to the shop floor but the national headquarters carefully monitored shop floor activities. Company councils had been established in sixty of the concerns organized by the ASTMS, whose efficiency was said to rival the better managements. In 1978 it spent nearly £300,000 on publications and publicity and more than £50,000 on education.

With such organization Jenkins had plenty of time for political activities, to which he brought his organizational skills. The ASTMS Parliamentary Committee, of which he was secretary, had forty-two members, and in 1978 concerned itself with employment protection, industrial deafness, technological change, trade unionism in the armed forces, racial discrimination, genetic manipulation, the universities and EEC law. He had served on a number of other committees, including the Bullock Committee on Industrial Democracy. He was a member of the National Research Development Board and part-time board member of the British National Oil Corporation. When we met he was preparing to spend five weeks at the Woodrow Wilson Centre in the United States.

Whether or not corporatism could arrest the county's decline, and the assumption must be that it would develop into a single-party centralized state of a fascist nature, it was a logical development for the British trade union movement. The leaders believed that they were the representatives of the working class, the second nation with its own constitution (the rules and standing orders of the TUC) and its own parliament (the annual conference). This was seen or felt to give them a legitimacy and authority which, despite obeisances to the other constitution and parliament, rivalled the existing order.

It was of course an enormous confidence trick, and one can only wonder how they got away with it for so long. As already noted, much trade union power had been transferred to the shop floor. The general secretary of a large union could expect to help run the country, but not the union he claimed to represent. Only too often

* *White-Collar Unionsim: The Rebellious Salariat*. Routledge & Kegan Paul, 1979

87

his authority had been reduced to declaring official the unofficial strikes called by militant shop stewards. Despite the democratic organization of many unions, very few general secretaries represented the membership as a Member of Parliament represents his constituency. Most union elections were a farce because so few members bothered to vote, and unlike MPs general secretaries did not always have to seek reelection.

Once elected they could expect to have the job for life, and in effect they joined a self-perpetuating oligarchy. They became members of one of the estates of our quasi-corporative state; at least before the Tory victory of 1979. They were invited to 10 Downing Street to help resolve national crises over beer and sandwiches. Their block votes could sway Labour party conferences. The BBC and independent television companies, who apparently believed that Britain was already a corporate state, invited them to appear on programmes with Cabinet ministers and representatives of the Confederation of British Industry. To that extent they fared better than most politicians in opposition, and they could look forward to resuming their rightful place in our quasi-corporate state when Labour returned to office.

This was power by any standards, but the 1974 social contract was indisputable evidence that they were playing a confidence trick on the nation. First known as the social compact, it was renamed presumably to claim some historical legitimacy from the social contract of Hobbes, Locke and Rousseau. Intended to formalize the close corporative relationship between government and unions, the Labour government undertook to introduce specific social policies demanded by the TUC in return for an unspecified undertaking to modify wage demands. It worked only briefly, and wage settlements wildly exceeded official guidelines, but the wave of strikes in the early months of 1979 finally proved that the union members could not keep their side of the bargain. Another contract was quickly drawn up. Known as the concordat, it suggested that the TUC had assumed the spiritual authority of the Holy See after conceding, if only privately, the loss of its temporal powers; but when the Labour government was defeated there was no reason to believe that the TUC could keep any bargain even when wearing the triple tiara.

The confidence trick could not work because of the inner contradictions of the trade union movement. In a corporate state each estate must have the authority to speak for the people it represents. The TUC would be expected to help increase productivity by imposing industrial discipline, by accepting new technologies and removing restrictive practices. It would have to work within the law and modify free collective bargaining.

In the planned society of a corporate state, or Scargill's Marxist state, wages would be as much the concern of the planners as the allocation of resources. Free collective bargaining can only work, at least in theory, in the hard and cold world of Mrs. Thatcher and her monetarist advisers. The unions would of course have to accept the consequences, such as fewer jobs for higher pay and other aspects of the market economy.

This is the logic of free collective bargaining which the unions have managed to ignore, and the country has been forced to pay the price of higher wages and continuing low productivity. Part of the price has been inflation, but unions with muscle have managed to negotiate wage increases above the inflation rate. When this has led to disaster, when an industry has priced itself out of the market and factories have been threatened with closure, the unions have demanded government intervention. Jobs for all has been the watchword, whether or not the men and women employed have created sufficient wealth or provided a good service.

*

The best-known exponent of the con trick was Jack Jones, the former general secretary of the Transport and General Workers' Union. He was a dour man, with an honesty that some people found disconcerting. One could not imagine him making a joke to ease a tense situation or telling a little white lie to avoid embarrassment. We first met at a reception in Buckingham Palace – a royal confirmation of our quasi-corporate state – and even in a black tie he managed to look the stereotype proletarian. I assumed that he had left his cloth cap in the cloakroom. He was uncompromising in his working-class attitudes, and was still living in a council flat when he became a Companion of Honour.

The con trick was eventually to be his downfall, but for many years he was regarded as the most powerful man in Britain. A slight exaggeration, but a private secretary who was present when Jones met Edward Heath at 10 Downing Street remembered years later how he radiated power. He was the main architect of the social contract, and his hand could be seen in legislation that followed.

Jones was born on Merseyside, and began his working life in the docks. He was active in Labour politics and was secretary of the local ward when he was only sixteen. He became the youngest member of Liverpool City Council. Tough and tenacious, and with a passion for social justice, he probably could have gone far in politics but chose union work.

He was appointed district secretary for Coventry, where his wife was a shop steward, and proved to be a shrewd negotiator and successful recruiter. He was already interested in industrial democracy, and encouraged shop-floor bargaining despite opposition from employers and other union officials. It was probably the beginning of the transfer of power from general secretaries to shop stewards, although this was contested by some trade unionists because he reasserted his authority from time to time. For instance, with the help of Hugh Scanlon, the leader of the engineers' union, he settled the Ford strike in 1971 over the heads of the strike committee.

Jones was not always liked by his colleagues, perhaps because he was dour and uncompromising, but promotion was inevitable. He was appointed assistant executive secretary in 1963 and general secretary six years later. In between, he joined the National Executive Committee of the Labour party and numerous other bodies. He was also associated with the Institute for Workers' Control and *The Tribune*, the voice of the Labour left, which enhanced his reputation as a radical.

It was well deserved, but he was more of a populist than a Marxist. He really believed that ordinary working people were capable of inheriting the earth, of running industry and the country. There can be no argument about that, but I suspect that he was also a romantic. He was christened James Larkin after the Liverpool Irish socialist, and growing up on Merseyside he must have responded to the romantic working-class view of Irish nationalism. Certainly in later life he was known to quote Connolly and Pearse, the socialist poets and martyrs of the Easter Rising. True or simply ridiculous, he had a vision of life that could not only have been fed by dreary socialist manifestos. One could argue that his dream of industrial democracy was essentially romantic.

His vision took him to the centre of national power, and unlike some of his colleagues he believed in the social contract. He was determined to keep his side of it, but the transfer of power to the shop floor, which he had encouraged if not initiated, was his undoing. After persuading the TUC to accept wage restraint, he was repudiated eventually at a TGWU conference by delegates and shop stewards who did not share his view of industrial democracy.

It was perhaps a romantic approach to building motor cars, and it almost ruined the industry. Much of the evidence was collected by the Central Policy Review Staff, and published in a report entitled *The Future of the British Car Industry** The statistics were

* HMSO, 1975

unarguable. In 1955 Britain accounted for more than a quarter of world production outside the United States, and only one tenth in 1975. In 1965 it had 95 percent of the British market, and 65 percent in 1975. (It fell to about 40 percent by 1979.) The CPRS identified many causes for this competitive weakness, which of course became worse in subsequent years. They included poor distribution, quality and delivery, insufficient investment, high manufacturing costs and bad labour relations. Management could not escape its share of responsibility, nor could successive governments with their stop-go policies, but Jack Jones' and Hugh Scanlon's men did their best to bring down British Leyland and Chrysler.

For instance, because of labour disputes and restrictive practices British productivity per man was far below the levels in EEC plants. Even when assembling the same car, and working with identical capital equipment, nearly twice as many men were required in British plants. The work pace was slower, due to slower production line speeds, late starts, frequent stoppages and bad work practices. Maintenance was also poor. British plants employed 50 to 70 percent more maintenance men than continental plants, yet lost twice as many production hours due to breakdowns.

Labour disputes were ten times as many as in British industry generally, and even higher compared to EEC car plants. The fragmented union structure provoked many disputes over recruitment and demarcation, and when agreements were reached management could never be certain that the unions and shop stewards could carry them out. As a result, the British car industry failed to achieve continuity of production and was obliged to spread the cost of capital equipment over much fewer units than EEC companies. It could not guarantee delivery and therefore lost orders.

The CPRS report was ignored. The government was too busy rescuing Chrysler from bankruptcy, and the unions would have nothing to do with it. Production continued to deteriorate as Stephen Fay of *The Sunday Times* discovered when he enquired into labour relations in the continental and British plants of the Ford Motor Company. It produced the same cars on the same machines in a number of countries. The only major variable factor was labour, and in 1978 it took 9.5 Britons to build an Escort at Halewood and only 4.1 West Germans at the Saarlouis plant. One British worker at Dagenham produced 110 doors for Cortinas while a Belgian worker at Genk produced 240.

One reason for the startling differences in the production rates was that the continental managements were allowed to manage.

In West Germany, for instance, management and the unions were represented on supervisory boards, and there were elected works councils, but management fixed work standards and decided how fast the production lines ran. In Britain, Fay reported, the unions were proud of the power they had gouged out of traditional management prerogatives. Bernard Passingham, the leading Transport and General Workers steward at Dagenham, spoke fondly of a press in the plant which had not been worked for seven years because the workers considered the machine unsafe. Another machine, which cost £1m, stood idle for eight months while the stewards negotiated manning levels.

Bill Collard, the senior manager for Dagenham, said that the unions were getting deeper and deeper into the management process. Albert Caspers, a West German manager in Liverpool, said, 'We put in a machine that could save ten jobs, and we're lucky if the unions give us three. They just don't believe in change; they just say "we can't work that". No wonder the British engineers are depressed.'

Having acquired the power to share in management decisions the stewards refused to accept their share of the responsibility. Continuous production of vehicles requires a large measure of industrial discipline, and serious lapses such as persistent absenteeism should carry penalties. Fay discovered that this presented few problems to Ford managers on the continent, where the unions accepted dismissal if the established procedure had been followed. Not so in Britain, where shop stewards refused to abide by agreements they had helped to negotiate.

Passingham said that his job was only to get his men a better deal, and did nothing when some men walked off the job after one of their mates had been disciplined. As a consequence, Dagenham suffered 208 such disputes in 1977, leading to the loss of 2,508,786 man-hours and 61,254 vehicles. The final result of course was lower wages for British workers, increased penetration of the home market by foreign makes, and the further improverishment of the nation. At the time of writing, British Leyland and Chrysler (renamed Talbot) survived only because of government assistance. A large proportion of the proceeds from North Sea oil and gas was being used to pay for imported cars and Jones' version of industrial democracy.

This does not mean that industrial democracy cannot work in Britain, although the Ford experience is not reassuring. Bob Ramsey, who was in charge of labour relations, told Fay that 'after the strikes in 1969 and 1971 we decided we had to manage by consent... The first thing we did was to get the bargaining arrangements right. We wanted to negotiate a wage deal every two years, and we wanted to deal with negotiators who could deliver the goods, so the shop stewards joined the National Joint Negotiating Committee.

'Then we set up sub-committees involving our plant convenors to deal with work standards, pensions, training, trade union membership (we conceded a post-entry closed shop). We allowed a five-day *status quo* period in the event of disagreements, and our procedures meant that disputes could be settled quickly, within the plants. Next we increased worker participation. Ours might not be a great experiment, but we have tried to keep workers informed during negotiations by putting out leaflets entirely devoid of propaganda. We wanted to open the books, and our chairman now sees the NJNC and 130 trade union representatives twice a year to discuss our prospects.

'We also tried to get a new discipline agreement to deal with emotive issues like dismissal, and we proposed independent compulsory arbitration in cases where we could not agree. The unions rejected that so we offered non-compulsory arbitration. But the engineering union turned it down, and since all our agreements have to be unanimous, we have had to drop it. The objection was to the principle of discipline, but it's ironic because we are the people who are trying to give rights away. All the things the unions have said we ought to do, we've done. I didn't quarrel with giving them what they wanted; that's OK. But you've got to have some response from them, and we've had no response.'

*

Eric Wigham, the industrial writer, once recalled that as the 1930s drew towards their close the fame of Britain's orderly and peaceful system of industrial relations spread abroad. This persuaded two Americans, Frank Gannet, the owner of a chain of newspapers, and Professor B. F. Catherwood, to come to see how we did it, and afterwards they published a series of articles on the way the system worked.

'While we in America have had increased strife between employer and employee in industry, the British have been blessed with little of this conflict between capital and labour,' Gannet explained in the introduction. 'This prompted me to visit England to learn why the country had so few strikes and why industrial peace there generally prevails ... I observed a zeal and enthusiasm on the part of the employees such as one does not always see in (the United States). Supervisors or superintendents were scarce. Every man was diligently at work, never loafing, never killing time. All were as busy as beavers, trying to turn out a full

93

day's work.'*

No doubt many people will now read that excerpt with disbelief, and Wigham wryly added that after the war many accounts of a similar state of affairs in the United States were published in Britain. Nevertheless, an equal number of people probably believe that industrial peace was normal before the second world war. I have met some who looked back with nostalgia to what they thought were the good old days when trade union leaders and members were good honest chaps who knew their place.

That peaceful period was in fact only a truce which followed the surrender of the trade union movement to the constitutional government after the failure of the General Strike in 1926. To gain a proper perspective of the history of industrial relations in this country, I suggest that it should be seen as a second Hundred Years War. Certainly it has been waged on and off since the strikes and lock-outs of the great depression of the 1870s, and the two world wars were the only other periods of truce.

Trade unionism in one form or another began long before the 1870s. As with other British institutions, its roots reach far back in our past. Journeymen combined against guild masters in the sixteenth and seventeenth centuries, and skilled workers such as weavers and printers formed trade societies in the following century. They were seldom interfered with while they remained local societies; indeed, they enjoyed some legal protection under the Elizabethan Statute of Artificers until the Combination Acts made them illegal. These were repealed in 1824, but other repressive laws remained. The Tolpuddle Martyrs were not prosecuted for combining, but for administering unlawful oaths.

Their transportation to Australia accelerated the growth of the movement, and within a few years attempts were made to form non-craft unions open to all workers. Some also became political in the accepted sense of the word, and agitated for electoral reform. Widespread industrial action followed the first Reform Act of 1832 which left them unfranchised.

The Grand National Consolidated Trades' Union, organized by Robert Owen, was the first attempt to unite the various trade societies. It quickly collapsed, as did the subsequent National Association of United Trades for the Protection of Labour, but the Trades Union Congress was successfully established in 1868. Legal status was achieved with the Trade Union Act of 1871, and was strengthened by subsequent legislation. Employers began to recognize and bargain with them, but the gains were lost during the depression of the 1870s, and this was followed by the rise of

* *Strikes and the Government 1893–1974.* Macmillan, 1976

what G. D. H. Cole described as the new unionism, in part the product of socialist agitation. The Hundred Years War had begun.

One early decisive battle was fought by the new unionism in Taff Vale, where the dismissal of a signalman by the local railway company led to a strike. The general manager sought an injunction against the Amalgamated Society of Railway Servants and claimed damages for breach of contract. The case went to the House of Lords, which in 1901 decided that a trade union was liable to damages for the actions of its members.

Damages were fixed at £23,000 and costs at about £19,000, which were immense sums in those days, but much more was at stake. The decision meant that any union involved in a strike risked having to pay unlimited damages, and in effect it threatened to deny workers their main protection against exploitation. The unions' response was immediate, and its pressure tactics contributed to the Liberal victory in the 1906 elections. The Labour Representation Committee drafted a Bill, upon which the Trade Disputes Act of 1906 was largely based. It made peaceful picketing lawful and gave unions what Sidney Webb described as 'an extraordinary and unlimited immunity however great the damage caused and however unwarranted the act!*' It was nothing less than monstrous, he added.

This immunity was the foundation upon which union power, monstrous or otherwise, was to be built. More battles followed. The movement moved to the left during the first world war, when the shop stewards came into their own. The General Strike led to the Trades Disputes Act of 1927. Union immunity was somewhat restricted but the then Tory Prime Minister, Stanley Baldwin, was anxious to bind up the nation's wounds, which helps to explain the period of relative peace reported by the visiting Americans. The restrictions were removed after the second world war and the movement emerged as the powerful force we know today.

Oddly enough, a Tory, Walter Elliot, was the first to recognize it as such. Speaking from the front bench in 1951, Elliot said, 'A new entity has emerged in the body politic, the power of trade unions to intervene in an organized fashion in our lives, either to promote or to bring to a dead stop the intricate processes upon which a modern state depends. Accompanying that is a sense of a new kind of property – property in a job. Are we not witnessing the emergence of a new Estate of the Realm – a new strand in our national make-up lacking which the nation cannot work. It is the hallmark of an Estate of the Realm that it can vote supplies. We can vote the supply of money, without which enterprises of the State cannot be conducted; the trade unions can vote the supply of

* Ibid

95

labour without which, equally, the affairs of the State cannot be conducted.'

Trade unions had cause to be proud at the time. Despite immense opposition and hardship, they had created a genuine working-class movement and earned the right to speak for organized labour. It was a pioneer movement, an example for all the workers of the world. They had added another dimension to the democratic process without which political democracy could not have achieved the large if still incomplete measure of social justice now enjoyed by the majority. To that extent, it was a power for good, for the country as well as its membership, but at the end of the hundred years of struggle the fruits of victory were often bitter.

In recent years the movement has done more damage to the economy and the country than any other of Elliot's estates of the realm, and has achieved less for its members than trade unions in other industrial democracies. The reasons are various: the ramshackle structure of the movement, the undisciplined shop steward system, competition between unions recruiting members working in the same industry or plant, demarcation disputes and the reluctance to accept new technologies. Some unions are now beginning to look like a Luddite movement, apparently determined to perpetuate an obsolete industrial system.

It has also become an economically illiterate movement. Few of the general secretaries who accept a mixed economy, at least in theory, understand the necessity for profits. Fewer of the rank and file accept the social wage – health and welfare services, unemployment and family benefits, to mention only a few items – as part of payment for their labour. Far fewer understand, or want to understand, that wealth must be created before it can be shared. The movement generally is mainly interested in jobs, which is understandable, but not any kind of job whether or not it is productive or provides an essential service.

The movement has also created a demeaning and destructive caste system comparable to the system which over the centuries made India a backward country riven with injustice and inequality. The newspaper industry is the obvious example. The employees of Times Newspapers Ltd. belong to eight unions. These are the main castes comparable with the *Brahman*, *Kshatrya*, *Vaisya* and *Sudra* castes, but more numerous. The British newspaper castes are no less rigid. With the exception of the National Union of Journalists, they are closed castes; and unlike in Hinduism a man cannot be elevated to a higher caste by following the path of duty, devotion or knowledge.

Within the eight main castes, there are more than sixty sub-castes known as chapels. They are not nearly as numerous as Indian sub-castes, but again are completely closed. Each has its own work which cannot be performed by another sub-caste. For instance, when pages are being made up in the composing room, a journalist cannot touch type; that is the prerogative of the stonehand, who in turn cannot pull a proof. That is the right of the proofpuller. The sub-castes are also self-governing. The father or mother of the chapel is the *munsif*, *diwan* or *sipahi*, and the chapel committee the *panchayat*.

Their authority is far-reaching; for instance, if I want a secretary the application is made to the clerical section of the National Society of Operative Printers, Graphical and Media Personnel, which provides one. Little or no effort is made to find out what work has to be done. On one occasion when I wanted a temporary secretary, I was sent a girl who could not type and then another who said that she would only answer the telephones. Nearly a month passed before a suitable secretary arrived. The caste system prevents managers from managing, increases costs, delays production and has led to constant interruptions with loss of issues or copies. Only one sub-caste has to withdraw its labour to bring production to a standstill. It also increases inter-union rivalry which is endemic throughout the movement.

Trade union unity, of which the movement is proud, is only skin deep. In fact, unions unite only in defence of their immunities. Otherwise each union fights for what are seen as its own interests and regardless of the damage done to other unions. The strong unions invariably win, and at a cost greater than that inflicted upon the trade union movement. In their rush to get their snouts in the trough, to quote Sid Weighell of the National Union of Railwaymen, the weak, the sick and the old go to the wall. The obvious example is the great suffering caused by recent strikes of hospital and other public service unions. The picketing of hospitals denied treatment to the seriously ill and must have shortened their lives and ended some. Lonely old people were made more miserable by the denial of the meals-on-wheels service. Human compassion, which motivated the trade movement in the early years, has become a casualty of union power.

The past is responsible for many of our union troubles. The West German system is rational, efficient and humane because it was reorganized after the second world war by men such as Vic Feather of the TUC who was fully aware of the mistakes made during the haphazard growth of his own movement, but the incomes policies of the post-war years had damaging consequences, not least when union leaders tried loyally to cooperate with the government. They took on more than they could deliver, and the result was indiscipline, or mutiny, in their own ranks and more power for militants. Inflation has also wreaked great damage, and to that extent our political masters are as guilty as the union masters.

The unions must clearly put their own house in order if they are to become a force for good again. Hateful as the word may sound, the only remedy is discipline and without it we cannot achieve a new equilibrium in British society. This will first require internal discipline such as the prevention of unofficial stoppages and strikes. Much could be achieved with disputes procedures and labour contracts. These are simple and well-tried methods, and there is no reason why they cannot be adapted to British conditions.

Trade union leaders will also have to accept some limitation on their political ambitions. Their movement is too big and now potentially destructive to remain largely outside the law. Given the disciplines acceptable in comparable and more successful industrial democracies, their Hundred Years war could still win a belated victory with fruits to be shared by all of us.

SIX

True Blue

I met Lord Home in the Carlton Club, an appropriate place to begin an enquiry into the Conservative party. Disraeli regarded the club as the social citadel of Toryism, and it had been intimately connected with the party leadership since it was founded in 1832. In the early days the whips worked with its political committee, and together performed functions which have long since passed to the party's Central Office. The Carlton was once credited with a mysterious and even sinister influence in the affairs of party and country, but the 1922 Committee, which represents the backbenchers and to that extent is a check on the leadership, commemorates a meeting at the club when the so-called Die-Hards rebelled against those leaders who wanted to remain in the Lloyd George coalition government.

Home was his usual easy-going and threadbare self. He was and always had been completely without side, perhaps because he was the fourteenth belted Earl of Home until he unbelted himself. Some people resented this aristocratic classlessness, sensing a suggested superiority too obvious to be clothed in arrogance and a good suit. Others thought that aristocrats in general and Home in particular had nothing to boast about, and in one of his self-deprecating moments he might have agreed.

Home had earlier lunched with the Archbishop of Canterbury, which might have been why he expressed concern about the loss of religion. He thought that it must have led to the weakening of moral standards, and might explain, at least in part, the national decline. How else could football hooliganism be explained? He was also worried about the welfare state. Perhaps there were not many scroungers but they were not good for morale, especially among the lower-paid. The welfare state had probably also weakened personal discipline.

In retrospect he thought that Butskellism had been wrong. The Tories had had to move to the middle ground, but they had probably given too much away on the welfare state and the unions. The outlook was not encouraging. Labour had exhausted its ideas and the Tories had a great deal of thinking to do.

Meanwhile politics had become an auction, with each of the major parties offering more than they could possibly deliver. Again it was understandable, but he occasionally wondered how the Tories ever won an election.

It said something about Home that he could thus wonder aloud to a journalist, although his old critics in the party could wonder why he had hoped to win the 1964 election. Home had succeeded Harold Macmillan when ill-health forced him to resign in 1963, and he was not the party's first choice. The majority of the Cabinet preferred R. A. Butler and the constituency workers Lord Hailsham; but Macmillan advised the Queen to summon Home, who renounced his earldom, fought a by-election in a safe constituency and entered the Commons as Sir Alec Douglas-Home. (He accepted a life peerage when he retired from active politics in 1974.)

Home's tenure at 10 Downing Street was the shortest in recent history, although he might have won the 1964 election had he led a united party. Instead, Iain MacLeod and Enoch Powell, then the brightest of the rising younger Tories, refused to serve under him; and MacLeod condemned his appointment as a victory for the party establishment. Others dismissed Home as a political anachronism.

This was not altogether fair. Home had had considerable experience in government, as Parliamentary Private Secretary to Neville Chamberlain when he was Prime Minister, Minister of State at the Scottish Office, Minister at the old Commonwealth Office and Foreign Secretary. He was a capable Foreign Secretary because he understood power, and knowing that Britain had little power acted accordingly. Britain would be a better place if all its political leaders were as straightforward and honest as Home. That said, he was the choice of the party's old establishment, and his love of grouse shooting and salmon fishing was seen to suggest a way of life completely divorced from modern Britain. His devotion to field sports was such that he camped out at No 10, or so it was said. His suitcases were rarely emptied because every Friday he and his wife caught the night train to Scotland to shoot or fish.

His honesty could embarrass the party. He once admitted that he knew little or nothing about economics, and joked that he could only count with the aid of matchsticks. The face and manner revealed the simplicity; the skin tight over the small round head, the eyes steady and friendly, the quickness with which he answered complicated questions as if the world could be divided into black and white, right and wrong. He was the last of the old Tories to get to the top, and his going marked the end of an era in the history of the party.

It has had many since it first emerged as a parliamentary faction in the eighteenth century. Some romantics go back to the previous century and seek its origins in the Civil War or in the struggle over the Exclusion Bill during the reign of Charles II; others from the decline of Jacobitism and the acceptance of the Revolutionary Settlement and the House of Hanover. One thing is certain, the faction acquired the name Tory at the time of the Exclusion Bill. Their opponents lampooned them as Tories, a name originally applied to Irish Catholic rebels who were also known as robbers and bogtrotters. Not to be outdone, the Tories dismissed the petitioners for the Bill as Whigs, which was derived from the whiggamores who were Scottish rebels.

The Tories have always regarded themselves as the party of Church and King, and until recently also saw themselves as the embodiment of the nation. This was a large claim, and historians would be hard pressed to prove it, even if they ignored ordinary Englishmen, which they do with the greatest of ease, and the pseudo-mysticism which went with the Tory belief of innate superiority. Ian Gilmour* nevertheless had a go by listing themes apparent in the writings of those he regarded as the fathers of Conservatism.

They got the idea of trimming from George Savile, Marquis of Halifax (1635–95), who believed that the Church, the Law and God Almighty Himself were trimmers. Conservatives earlier trimmed in favour of the state against *laissez-faire*, and today against the state and in favour of the individual. They trimmed to achieve balance. From David Hume (1711–76) they inherited scepticism, the sense of fallibility of human reason, and also the instinct for enjoyment. They agreed with the philosopher that the aim of statesmanship was the public benefit.

Edmund Burke (1729–97) gave them reverence for the nation, national institutions and national continuity; prudence and the necessity of complexity if freedom was to be preserved. Samuel Taylor Coleridge (1772–1834) taught them that misery and hardship could not be shrugged off by the state or by the well-to-do as the inevitable results of quasi-divine economic laws and forces. From Benjamin Disraeli (1804–81) they got the idea that the duty of the Tory party was to be national, and that its over-riding objectives were the preservation of national institutions and the improvement of the condition of the people. If the country's institutions were defective, the condition of the people would deteriorate; and if too little was done to safeguard or improve the living conditions of the people, the national institutions would be

* *Inside Right: A Study of Conservatism*. Hutchinson, 1977

endangered.

These and other writers, Gilmour concluded, profoundly believed in the rule of law and in civil and political liberty, and they knew that law and liberty could only be preserved if they were buttressed by private property. For them balance, prudence and moderation were cardinal political virtues, and tranquility and national unity primary political objectives. They were all acutely aware of the crucial importance of 'circumstance'.

Gilmour seemed to be suggesting that the Tories embodied all the virtues as well as the nation, which even a fellow Old Etonian might question, let alone somebody such as myself. If they were so concerned about the condition of the people they hardly demonstrated it during the thirties. I was only a kid at the time, but I have abiding memories of the hunger marchers slogging along the Victoria Embankment to Westminster, and of ragged dockers lining up outside dock gates in hope of a half-day's work. There are no chips on my shoulder, at least I do not think so, but I cannot forgive them for that. Times have changed, but they were always the party of landed interests and the bosses and before the rise of trade union power were generally as ruthless and selfish as our less-lovable union leaders and shop stewards.

They are still very much the party of the rich, the well-to-do and the bosses. Of course, some bosses vote Labour and a minority of trade unionists and their wives vote Tory. To that extent British society has not been completely polarized. The class battle lines have been fudged. There are also more natural Tories in England than in the Celtic fringe. If the Union was dissolved; if, for instance, England, Scotland, Wales and Northern Ireland became independent countries within the EEC, the Conservatives would be the dominant English party. Apart from such drastic surgery, many Tories hoped that the 1979 election was a portent for the future, that if the skilled and semi-skilled workers who voted Tory could be persuaded to drop or modify their abiding working-class attitudes Disraeli's hopes for a truly national party could be realized.

Those hopes are unlikely to be realized. Too many Tories live in constitutencies such as Abingdon and Arundel, Harrogate and Hove, Wirral and Worcester. Too many live in comfortable houses and not tower blocks. They send, or would prefer to send, their children to public or grammar schools and not comprehensives. Their speech is not always plummy, and the once fashionable lisp is now rare, except with posh socialists such as Roy Jenkins, but they have only to open their mouths in places such as Liverpool and Tower Hamlets to be instantly recognized as intruders.

High taxation and death duties have reduced the living standards of most if not all of them. Some forgo foreign vacations and other pleasures to put their children through public school, but we do not have to weep for them. Statistically at least, the redistribution of wealth has not got that far and even if it had, I for one would not be sorry. Even a modest measure of inherited wealth, or a kindly uncle or maiden aunt, can provide a cushion against adversity which the likes of me have never enjoyed. Worsthorne's Spaghetti Junction still applies. As for the rich, they still manage to look better off even than their richer American cousins. Perhaps it is the tailoring or the lingering assumption of superiority; whatever the reason, many of them can still raise the ire of their countrymen.

I was recently reminded of this almost physical separateness, the like of which was rarely evident during my years in the United States, at a cocktail party in one of those pleasant Georgian houses in Smith Square, Westminster. The House was still sitting but about half of the Tory front bench was present, and some were already wearing black ties presumably because they were going on to dinner parties. A few of the men looked as if they had just emerged from a hot bath. They were freshly shaved and pomaded, and the faces above the glasses of malt whisky, which they preferred to the proffered champagne, beamed self-confidence and well-being. They were among their own. They had gone to the same schools and universitites, and belonged to the same clubs. Despite the post-war social revolution, they were still members of a caste. No wonder the senior ICS men were once known as white Brahmins.

Some Americans had this separateness; I am thinking not of New York's café society or the so-called beautiful people, but the families long established on the eastern seaboard from New England to Virginia. They also went to private schools and old universities, and their clubs can be more exclusive than those in St. James's. They can be proud of their families in a way which would be regarded as snobbishly archaic in Britain. They can be recognized as easily as posh Tories although the giveaway signs are more subtle: the accent in Boston, the suggestion of horsiness in Albemarle county, Virginia, the button-down shirts and natural-shoulder suits from Brooks Brothers. As with those ICS men in India, the Bostonians have also been known as Brahmins and in the Old Dominion cultivated men and women are proud of being FFVs, or First Families of Virginia. Nevertheless, they do not obtrude presumably because they are citizens of the world's oldest social democracy.

It is entirely different in Britain where Tory separateness re-enforces class divisions. I am sure that some of them are as aware as is Arthur Scargill of the gap between 'them' and 'us', and would have it otherwise. Some obviously would not, and can be overbearing and nasty. They appear to believe, judging from conversations in the lobbies of Conservative party conferences and at board luncheons in the City, that Britain will not be great again until the death penalty and conscription are reintroduced and militant shop stewards arraigned as traitors.

Political opponents have made much of this general nastiness, but the party has not gone the way of the Liberals because, as Gilmour suggested, it has learned to trim. Indeed, over the decades the party has often been flexible and accommodating. Widespread anti-Semitism did not prevent Disraeli, an apostate Jew, from becoming leader of the party. Heath was the son of a local builder and Thatcher, the daughter of a grocer, became Britain's first woman Prime Minister. The first black Prime Minister could well be a Tory.

This must help to explain why between 1945 and 1979 the party was in power for about half of those 34 years, and could be in power until 1984. Class might still be the bane of British life, but privilege and separateness did not offend the majority of voters; or perhaps the majority found them no more offensive than the extreme Left of the Labour party and bullying trade unionists.

The Tories of course have another explanation for their survival, and it goes beyond Gilmour's romantic claims. They believe that they were born to rule, that they are the natural leaders of the nation. They have obviously had more experience as a party and a class, but their post-war record is not a proud one.

*

A party apologist could argue that they had some bad luck. Churchill was old and ill when he returned to Downing Street in 1951. He had earlier suffered two strokes and was to suffer more. He was an heroic figure commanding almost universal respect and affection, but by clinging to office too long he disrupted the natural processes of advancement with disastrous consequences when Anthony Eden finally became Prime Minister.

Eden also commanded respect and affection, and not only because of his charm and good looks. His resignation from office in 1938 commended him to the liberal-minded in all parties, and he was rightly regarded as an expert on foreign affairs. This was proved once again in 1954 when the French National Assembly rejected the idea of a European Defence Community. John Foster Dulles had threatened an agonizing reappraisal of the American commitment to the defence of Europe if the treaty was not ratified, and the future of the alliance was in doubt.

Eden, then Foreign Secretary, saved the day by skilfully negotiating agreements ending the occupation of West Germany, providing for West German and Italian membership of Nato and
confirming the American commitment. It was an extraordinary
diplomatic *coup*, but Britain had to pay a heavy price by promising
to garrison four army divisions and a tactical air force in West
Germany. Britain could not afford such a commitment, which
together with the massive rearmament programme launched by
the previous Labour government at the time of the Korean war,
was to prevent the necessary reorganization and improvement of
industry, but Eden's reputation was further advanced.

It did not survive after he finally became Prime Minister. He had
been the Crown Prince too long. He was ill, and his judgement
might have been affected. Whatever the reason, he apparently believed that Britain was still a great power and with France ordered
the invasion of Egypt. The Suez operation was an unmitigated disaster and Eden, ill again and distraught, resigned.

That party apologist would hardly be convincing. These diplomatic and military adventures proved that the Tory leadership did
not understand, or could not accept, that Britain was not one of the
great powers except in the fantasy world of allied diplomacy.
Worse, despite their connexions with the City of London, their
financial and economic management was equally disastrous. The
economy was not in bad shape in the early post-war years. Much
had to be done to drag it into the mid-twentieth century, but West
Germany and Japan had yet to recover from the war and Britain
and the United States still had a sellers' market. As Croham suggested, we might have made a go of it if both Labour and the Conservatives had not shared the illusion of being a great power.

Alas, when the Tories came to power in 1951 they were confron-
ted with a deficit in the balance of payments of about £700m,
largely because of the Korean war. Butler, the new Chancellor of
the Exchequer, panicked and ordered the first 'stop' of the 'stop-
go' policies which were to bedevil the economy in future years.
The panic was quite unnecessary because unnoticed by Butler and
the Treasury knights the economy was moving back into balance.
Butler was only the first of Tory Chancellors who, in the words of
Sam Brittan, 'were not merely innocent of economic complexities
but ... did not even have the practical financial flair that one
might reasonably expect from a party with business links.'*

The Tories were more successful in pursuit of consensus politics. The welfare state was allowed to continue because they
trimmed, in part to please the majority of voters but also because

* *Post-War Britain: A Political History*. Alan Sked & Chris Cook. Penguin 1979

of the social conscience of the party's liberal wing. Butler, who represented that wing, sought to win the middle ground as did Gaitskell, the Labour moderate. Hence Butskellism. There was nothing wrong with that. Natural justice as well as the understandable desire to remain in office required that the broad interests of the majority should be served. That is what political democracy is, or should be, all about. It was also a development of considerable importance in that the party of privilege did not try to put the clock back, apart from denationalizing steel and road haulage.

The Tories did the sensible thing, but their domestic policies were secondary to the role they wanted to play on the world stage. Like good army commanders, they wanted to keep the troops happy. Wartime rationing eventually came to an end, pensions were raised and the housing programme exceeded 300,000 units a year. For the first time in their lives most Britons began to enjoy a measure of affluence. Middle-class critics sneered at the so-called mini-culture, but not working-class families. Harold Macmillan, who succeeded Eden, was to say that they had never had it so good. He was right, but despite his political skills and genuine popularity he was arguably responsible for more of our present troubles than any other Prime Minister.

At the time it seemed that Macmillan was setting the country on the right course. His 'Wind of Change' speech did not only apply to Africa. A new equilibrium could have emerged, and with it that long-promised land fit for heroes, but it is not unfair to suggest that Macmillan personified much that was still wrong with Britain, and Tory Britain in particular, because he was very much part of the past from which he and the country were trying to escape.

Macmillan had served with gallantry in the first world war, and his wounds had left him more than the curious shuffling walk. With other sensitive survivors he was unable to forget, to use his own words, the killing of a generation. He first entered the House in 1924, and as Member for Stockton became sharply aware of the miseries of poverty and unemployment. He was a Tory social reformer before his time and advocated economic planning and a minimum wage. The indifference of the then leadership led him to say that 'a party dominated by second-class brewers and company promoters – a casino capitalism – is unlikely to represent anybody but itself'.

He was no less independent and courageous in his approach to foreign affairs. He renounced the party whip in protest against Baldwin's Abyssinian policy. None of this commended him to the leadership, and he spent many frustrated years on the back benches. Preferment came only after he became a member of the

Churchill group.

His appointment as Minister Resident in Algiers in 1942 was the first step forward. He got on splendidly with General Eisenhower, the Supreme Commander in North Africa, perhaps because he was half-American, and he proved to be an accomplished diplomat. When the Tories were returned to power in 1951 he was appointed in rapid succession to the Ministries of Housing and Defence, the Foreign Office and the Treasury. He supported Eden during Suez, but presumably because of that Tory facility for trimming gracefully reversed himself when he became Prime Minister.

Suez had dramatically and shamingly demonstrated that Britain was no longer a great power. Macmillan appeared to accept this but after his elevation let it be known that the alternative to Empire was not a Little England. The new foundation for British power was to be the special relationship with the United States, the growing Commonwealth and what was seen as Britain's commanding position in Europe. Macmillan told Eisenhower at their Bermuda meeting that 'you need us for ourselves, for the Commonwealth and as leader of Europe'. This was nonsense of course. The special relationship was beginning to look lop-sided, Britain could not speak for the new Commonwealth, General de Gaulle was still suspicious of the Anglo-American special relationship and in Bonn Dr. Konrad Adenauer was primarily concerned with relations with Paris and Washington. I was in Bonn when Reginald Maudling made the first approaches, and Adenauer was obviously unenthusiastic.

Macmillan persisted although in 1958 Britain's defence budget amounted to 8 percent of the GNP while West Germany was spending only half of that on raising the new Bundeswehr. It was crazy. Domestic spending was also rising, but unable to forget his Stockton experience Macmillan refused to cut spending despite rising inflation and the further weakening of sterling. No doubt he was also reluctant to do anything that would annoy the electorate, but one must assume that the past was the decisive factor. The Cabinet was divided; nevertheless, Macmillan was adamant and in January 1958 the Chancellor of the Exchequer, the then Peter Thorneycroft, and his two junior ministers, Enoch Powell and Nigel Birch, resigned.

Speaking in the House later, Thorneycroft said that we had gravely weakened ourselves by trying to do two things at the same time. We had sought to be a nuclear power and to maintain a welfare state. We had been trying to do that against a background of having to repay debts abroad equal to the whole of our existing reserves, of seeking to conduct an international banking business and of sustaining our position as one of the world's major oversea investors. These were not mean or unworthy things to wish to do, but it meant that always in the past twelve years there had been a crisis and the pound sterling had sunk from 'twenty shillings to twelve bob'. It was a picture of a nation in full retreat from its responsibilities.

To remain one of the world's major oversea investors when British industry was crying out for investment was not particularly worthy, but by refusing to observe the basic rules of fiscal and monetary prudence, Macmillan put Britain on the slippery slope. Many years later the *Spectator* said that without being fanciful one may date the disintegration of the currency from the day Thorneycroft's resignation was accepted. Previous Prime Ministers, including Attlee, had observed the rules and had stuck within a certain modest concept of the role of the state, but not Macmillan.

The indictment must stand, although at the time Macmillan dismissed the resignations as of no consequence and went off to practise higher diplomacy at foreign summits. He also supported the Concorde project in the fond hope that it would smooth the way of British entry into the EEC. Seventeen years later the bill for that *folie de grandeur* was in excess of £4,000m.

That was for the future of course. In the early sixties, Macmillan was still mesmerized by his concept of British power, and spent three-quarters of his time on foreign affairs and defence. He was determined to acquire Polaris submarines from the Americans to replace the obsolescent V-bombers. Kennedy, who had already suggested that Britain's place was in Europe, was at first reluctant. George Ball, the Under Secretary of State, was almost violently opposed, but at their meeting in Nassau in the Bahamas, Kennedy again fell under Macmillan's spell. They had previously met in Key West and Bermuda, and the President was captivated by the Edwardian charm. It was a quality sorely missed in his *ersatz* Camelot.

Macmillan had what can only be described as an avuncular relationship with Kennedy, who eventually decided that the old man was a nice guy and the United States should do what it could to help him. The meeting was held just before Christmas 1962. The sun was warm, but without being overly dramatic I felt a chill. I was dismayed although the files show that I reported the decision as objectively as I could. Back in Washington, Ball tried to retrieve the situation, but in January on the day Kennedy was to give his State of the Union message to Congress, de Gaulle blackballed Britain's entry into the EEC. The secure triangular future which Macmillan had planned for Britain disappeared in a momentary glow of world power.

*

The real decline of Britain, not only as a military and industrial power but as a country which had lost its way, began in the sixties. Earlier, for all the failures and disappointments, there had been the confident assumption that Britain would make it. That confidence was dissipated in the sixties, and for a steadily-growing minority of informed opinion the national decline began to look irreversible. Indeed, some took a queer kind of pride in the decline.

Nearly everybody I talked to during this enquiry agreed that Suez was the turning point. Many reasons were given, but I am convinced that Macmillan, who came to power after Suez, missed an opportunity rarely available to a Prime Minister – to turn the country round and set it on a new course. It is true that he rallied the country and party after Suez, but he could not shake off the fantasy of world power. That disaster led to others, not least after the short Home interregnum to Wilson's perpetuation of that fantasy for another six years. The Walter Mitty instinct of Wilson would have been inhibited, and less harm done, if MacMillan had faced up to reality. More attention could have been given to getting the economy right, to establishing a proper and honourable role for the trade unions, and to deciding the allocation of resources for social services.

There was of course no guarantee that Macmillan and Wilson would have succeeded. Perhaps the former's Edwardian manner accurately reflected the real man, probably Wilson was too kind and romantic to make a forceful Prime Minister. Perhaps there was something in the British character which made such decisive changes difficult if not impossible. Allowances must be made for such reservations: nevertheless, comparable industrial democracies made a go of it.

That said, the sixties were a difficult period for anybody in authority. Macmillan could have listened to Thorneycroft, but neither he nor Wilson could be held wholly responsible for the behaviour of the British people. The Profumo scandal was an obvious example. If it was a moral issue, as *The Times* asserted, it was one which mankind had lived with almost from the beginning of time. Neither Macmillan nor Wilson had any control over the social revolution which was then sweeping away much of the moral, social and religious baggage of the past.

But they could have realized that it did more than raise skirt hems and loosen sexual morals, that it had a political significance no less fundamental than the growing power of the trade unions.

Arguably the social revolution was the one post-war development to succeed in breaking with the past in that it finally swept away the residue of Bagehot's deferential society which had made the task of government so easy for so long.

Deference was a casualty of the second world war of course, but it took time and satirical programmes such as *Beyond the Fringe* and *That Was The Week That Was* to kill off much of the old acceptance of authority. Ministers had been savaged before, but not on television screens watched by millions of people. Macmillan was doubly vulnerable; apart from the Edwardian manner there were the inevitable trans-Atlantic comparisons. John Kennedy was not the greatest President since Lincoln, but his charisma was such that he dominated the imagination of many Britons. The Kennedy men saw themselves as the junior officers of the second world war who had come into their own, and not a moment too soon, while Britain was seen still to be ruled by old dugouts of the first world war.

The comparison was unfair, but as Kennedy once said, life was unfair. A great deal of nonsense was said and written about Kennedy, who was a flawed man, but the fact remained that a highly vocal and influential section of British society, as well as the young, signalled their discontent. They were discontented not only with MacMillan and then Wilson but with Westminster, Whitehall and the established order. To my knowledge, no politician recognized the significance of this bloodless revolution, but thereafter the decline of Britain was obvious.

It was not necessarily irreversible. A more realistic administration and a reasonably well-run economy could have worked wonders. Edward Heath seemed to understand this when the Tory Shadow Cabinet met at the Selsdon Park Hotel in Croydon in early 1970 to prepare for the next general election. It was an exciting occasion for the Tories, and not only because of the prospect of a return to power. The Conservative party was clearly going through another metamorphosis.

Men of privilege remained members of the party leadership. A few of the old knights of the shires were still prominent on the back benches; but power was moving into the hands of a new meritocracy, to men and women of what was once known as humble origins. Peter Walker was the outstanding example. Heath and Thatcher had at least gone to Oxford; Walker, the son of a factory worker who became a small shopkeeper, had left school when he was sixteen. To that extent, his origins were more humble than many Labour Members on the back as well as the front benches.

Walker was still under thirty when first elected to the House of Commons. He was tall and hungry-looking, and with an indeterminate chin. He would have passed unnoticed among the many thousands of City workers who surge over London Bridge every morning, but he had always been an ambitious political animal and had started very early. He was a founder member of the Young Conservatives in his constituency when he was thirteen, and was pointed in the right direction two years later by Leo Amery when they met at a party conference.

The old Tory gave him two words of advice. He should go to university to read books and learn to make conversation, and then make money before entering politics. Financial independence was essential for honourable politicians; without it he might have to compromise his principles because of a house mortgage and the demands of a growing family. Walker ignored the first but accepted the second. As with other penniless youngsters the local Carnegie library was his university, and over lunch one day he recalled how he went to the librarian and asked for basic books on all the political parties. He got a job as an insurance clerk because the only man in his street with a car was in insurance, and became a millionaire after he founded Slater Walker Securities with Jim Slater.

His background persuaded some Tories that Walker was the usual City spiv seeking respectability. Ambitious entrepreneurs were lauded on the City pages of *The Daily Mail* but not in the Smoking Room of the House of Commons. In fact, he got on well enough with the older Tories who might have been expected to dislike his kind. He listened to them as they sipped their whiskies or brandies. They might not have had high IQs, he decided, but they had been around a long time and had a broad view of history and politics. They also had a sense of public service. Nowadays, he added, the Smoking Room was filled with grey men drinking bitter lemon and discussing clauses of some obscure Bill in the hope of attracting the attention of the Whips.

He was to buy broad acres in Worcestershire, and might also have become a Tory knight (his MBE was the customary award for Young Conservative leaders) but his background explained why he became a Heath man. When Home decided to resign the leadership, he insisted, presumably because of the bad blood caused by the method of his elevation, that his successor must be elected. Walker became Heath's campaign manager, and was rewarded first with a place in the new Shadow Cabinet and then appointed the first Secretary of State for the Environment.

This was one of the new super-ministries run by so-called overlords. They were widely regarded as abominations, bureaucracy gone mad, and the subsequent reform of local government suggested that it was running amok. Walker defended this further extension of centralization. Modern life was too complicated for separate ministries such as Transport, which thought of nothing but providing roads for lorries without thinking about housing and the environment generally. It was conceded that he ran the new ministry efficiently, perhaps because unlike Crossman he did not just complain about the Civil Service.

From the beginning he decided that he alone would be in charge, and held meetings every morning with his Ministers of State to discuss the work of the ministry without minutes. The Permanent Secretary objected to his exclusion, and Walker said that he could attend as long as he could attend the meetings the Permanent Secretary had with his senior men. Walker won that battle, and afterwards regularly had all his top civil servants in for tea for similar informal discussions. They often stayed for dinner.

Aristocrats such as Home and Carrington were members of the new Tory Cabinet, but Walker as well as Heath personified what appeared to be the emerging new Toryism. Both had had humble beginnings, but they were very different. Walker was a natural politician and believed in the art of the possible. Heath, a born ship's captain, expected to be obeyed although he had told the admissions tutor at Balliol that he wanted to be a professional politician. He afterwards said, 'I started to be a politician at school. As a boy I didn't really think of myself as a Tory or anything else, but just as somebody political'. His upbringing in genteel Broadstairs might explain why he chose the Conservative party, but at Oxford he denounced the Munich Agreement and in an Oxford City by-election supported the Labour candidate.

After the war Heath was a temporary civil servant and then news editor of *The Church Times* before joining Brown, Shipley, the merchant bankers. He did not get rich, but made enough money to live well and run an expensive yacht. In 1950 he was elected as Member for Bexley, and promotion came quickly after he distinguished himself in the Whip's Office. He served in a number of ministerial posts, including Lord Privy Seal with special responsibility for negotiating Britain's entry into the EEC. De Gaulle's blackball did not damage his reputation for good sense and hard work.

Vic Feather, the trade union leader, saw a great deal of Heath when he was Minister of Labour, and said that he was always moderate and constructive. He was not politically motivated, and understood the need for conciliation. This changed when Heath became Prime Minister. As reported earlier, when Feather went to No 10, he was expected not to negotiate but to take orders with a touch of the forelock, an attitude which eventually made confrontation with the miners inevitable. Heath had always been stiff and

112

uneasy in company. Walker, who still greatly admired him, said that he had all the qualities of a great leader except that he could not get on with people and was impatient with the minutiae of politics. He was flawed, perhaps because he did not have a wife and children to deflate him from time to time.

There was probably more to it than that. At the 1970 Conservative party conference Heath said, 'Our purpose is to bring our fellow citizens to recognize that they must be responsible for the consequences of their own actions'. An admirable objective, but a political correspondent observed after his defeat that Heath did not seem to regard trade unionists as fellow citizens. William Whitelaw, Francis Pym and Lord Hailsham did, despite their very different backgrounds, and knew that they could only hope to rule by consent. Heath was also a disciple of Disraeli, he was a founder member of the One Nation Group, but was incapable of translating theory into practice. For all his intellectual and physical vigour, I think that he was crippled by his lower-middle class background.

I can attest as a former working-class lad that the gap between me and my mates and the lower-middle class made us suspicious of each other. I do not subscribe to the fond old Tory theory that the people at the top of the social heap get on well with those at the bottom. When I was growing up the gap was so wide that we did not even think of the well-born and powerful as fellow citizens, but the lower-middle class despised, perhaps even feared us. We were what they had been or might have been, but, as they probably saw it, for their hard work and thrift.

I have no way of proving that Heath was a victim of his upbringing; only the atavistic signals at the back of my mind whenever I met Heath, in his Albany flat, at summit and other international conferences, in the House of Commons and at ambassadorial dinners. I would not mention it here except that his successor as leader of the party, Margaret Thatcher, had the same kind of upbringing and did not seem to regard trade unionists as fellow citizens.

*

My first impression of Margaret Thatcher was of a good-looking woman who had worn well. She was then about fifty, and had recently been elected party leader after many years on the front bench. Heaven knows how many late sittings she had endured, but the face and throat were unlined and she looked like the stereotype middle-class competent Mum with a loving husband and a minimum of worries. It was one of those Fleet Street oc-

casions when leading politicians meet journalists over the lunch-
eon table to discuss affairs of the day. She had none of the
suspicion or resentful reserve of Heath. She joined easily in the
preliminary small talk, and afterwards was as candid in her replies
to questions as any journalist could expect a politician to be. She
gave as good as she got, and even sought advice on how to behave
on television. It could have been a womanly wile, but she knew
she was awful on the box and needed all the advice she could get.

My abiding impression was of a very determined woman who
thought that she knew where she was going, and was confident of
reaching her destination. This was doubly impressive because she
certainly knew that she would get only one chance. She knew that
the Tories, unlike the Labour party, were always loyal to their
leaders until they failed and then had no compunction in getting
rid of him or her.

She had helped to get rid of Heath. She had been his most candid
critic as Prime Minister because of the U-turns in policy, especially
the decisions to print money and rescue lame-duck firms to keep
down the unemployment figures. She was ready to join in the
backbench campaign to supplant him when the time came. Sir
Keith Joseph, a close frontbench colleague, refused to rise to the
challenge, and she announced her candidature for the leadership.
It was very bold of her; no woman had ever led a major British political party, and at the time her rivals appeared to be better placed.
No wonder that Heath afterwards refused to accept her leadership
and retired to the back benches.

She had come a long way from her father's grocer's shop in
Grantham, Lincolnshire. She had served behind the counter as a
child, attended chapel three times on Sunday and won a scholarship to the local grammar school. That led to Oxford where she
read chemistry and became president of the University Conservative Association. She married Denis Thatcher, a businessman
running a small family firm, and while raising two children used
what little spare time she had to read law and be called to the Bar.
She was adopted for the safe Tory seat of Finchley after contesting
two hopeless seats, was promoted to junior Minister within two
years and thereafter sat on the front bench.

Samuel Smiles would have smiled approvingly had he still been
alive, but approval was not universal. As party leader she was constantly out-manoeuvred by Wilson and Callaghan in the
Commons. Jim was especially good at putting her down, and her
occasional shrillness compared unfavourably with his practised
urbanity. Age-old prejudice still prevented many from accepting
her as a future Prime Minister, and support from feminists was not
forthcoming. They were prepared to burn their bras for the liber-

114

ation of women but her hair-do, twin-set and pearls, and the carefully modulated voice apparently offended them. They moved others to derision. She seemed to symbolise middle-class suburbia, although she lived in Chelsea, and a Britain widely assumed to have disappeared. Not the Britain of class privilege, but of the respectable poor and lower-middle class who still believed in self-help and standing on their own feet.

In fact they had not disappeared, but were largely ignored. They did not fit in the scheme of things envisaged by the Left, and for trendies they were figures of fun. They were more numerous than ever before, but once a measure of success had been achieved they tended to disappear without trace into the middle class. Many prominent men and women in all walks of life had begun in council flats and elementary schools, but rarely boasted about their achievements. This vanishing act was probably peculiar to Britain. Americans gloried in the myth of from log cabin to the White House; in fact very few Presidents had been born poor but the myth was not without foundation. Millions of ordinary Americans had made it and most of them, from corporation presidents to scientists and writers, were proud of it.

No such mythology existed in Britain although over the centuries British society had been the most mobile in Europe. The class lines looked rigid but they had been crossed by the bright and ambitious since the end of feudalism. They had been crossed more frequently in recent years, but once settled in their posh suburbs or apartment blocks few wanted to remember the mean streets and tenements from which they had come.

Perhaps some of them were not secure enough to boast about their transition, but there was another reason. A Jewish reviewer of my book *Growing Up Poor In London** expressed contempt for the poor *goyim* his family had left behind when they migrated from Whitechapel to Finchley or Golders Green. He was not expressing racial or religious arrogance, but the unsentimental view of those who had made it by their own efforts. Those left behind had not tried hard enough or were too inadequate or self-indulgent to try. They preferred to spend their time and money in the boozer and deserved what they got, or rather did not get.

This attitude, not necessarily selfish or insensitive, helped to explain the Heath and Thatcher approach to politics in general and the trade unions in particular. She was the more determined of the two. For all the talk about Selsdon man and rolling back the frontiers of government, Heath was a liberal compared with the so-called Iron Lady. She was determined to restore incentives for hard work and reward success as she and many like her had been

* Hamish Hamilton, 1973

115

rewarded. She passionately believed that liberty and trade, hard work and success, were sides of the same coin. It was no accident that somebody in the party's research department had rediscovered de Tocqueville.

This became clear during the run up to the 1979 election. The party manifesto was not undiluted Thatcherism; cautious minds had exercised some restraint, but it lambasted the Labour party for heaping privilege without responsibility on the trade unions thus giving a minority of extremists the power to abuse individual liberties and reduce Britain's chances of success. She was no less forthright about inefficient or spineless employers. She believed that more wisdom could be found in the boardroom than on the shop floor, but the Confederation of British Industry could not expect the kind of cozy relationship enjoyed by the TUC when Labour was in power. There would be no U-turns. They would have to stand up to the unions. The government would not fight their battles. The weak would go to the wall. The manifesto said that pay bargaining in the private sector should be left to the companies and workers concerned. At the end of the day, no one should or could protect them from the results of the agreements they made.

There was no doubt that she meant it, and one should not have been surprised. Women are supposed to be the weaker sex, but few Prime Ministers have been as tough as Golda Meir of Israel and Indira Gandhi of India. Thatcher was certainly tougher than any of her Cabinet colleagues.

*

The Central Office of the Conservative party in Smith Square was just across the way from the headquarters of the Labour party before the latter moved to Kennington. There was little to distinguish them from outside, two genteely shabby buildings which could house a variety of pressure groups looking for offices within walking distance of Parliament. They were very different inside. Transport House was wide open and visitors wandered about the corridors unaccompanied; the Tory Central Office gave the appearance of being under siege. The lobby was manned by uniformed security guards who might well have been trained by the White House police. Unlike Transport House, there was a suggestion of bustle, as if the place was filled with young ambitious executives and not tired party workers. The office of Ron Hayward, Labour's general secretary, looked like a boardroom; Lord Thorneycroft, the Tory chairman, worked in a smallish room reminiscent of a local bank manager's office.

116

Not surprisingly, the two men were also very different. Hayward, the self-proclaimed Cotswold peasant, spoke of the new Jerusalem without blushing. Thorneycroft was more urbane. He went to Eton, was a regular soldier and then a lawyer before entering Parliament in 1938. In his early days he was said to have looked like a musical comedy actor, but despite the suggestion of raffishness he was a superb parliamentarian. He out-witted Harold Wilson on more than one occasion, and could always be depended upon to wind up a major debate. In *Design for Freedom*, written ten years before he became Chancellor of the Exchequer, he tried to persuade Conservatives and Labour moderates to agree on common principles supporting individual enterprise and resisting the restrictive practices and monopoly power of employers and trade unions. He was one of the last of senior Ministers to resign over an issue.

This did not make him popular, and it was said that Macmillan invited him to rejoin the Cabinet in 1960 only because he wanted Enoch Powell who would not return without Thorneycroft. Some Tories were surprised when Thatcher appointed him party chairman in 1975, but she knew what she was doing. The last of the Churchill Cabinet still in active politics, he was a shrewd operator. Labour lost the election because of the winter of discontent, but Thorneycroft helped to increase the Tory majorities.

We met soon after the Tories had been returned to power, but he was not in a euphoric mood. He said that the electorate had not voted positively for the Tories, but simply because they felt that Labour was leading the country in the wrong direction. Not that a change of government was necessarily the answer, the national decline could not be reversed without a change of attitudes. The British disease was as much moral as economic. We were still a rich country, especially in coal and oil, but the British had lost their sense of purpose. The West Germans had discipline and the French a sense of national destiny, but the British now lacked both.

Too many had decided that it was easier to snatch wealth than to create it. The unions were not interested in productivity. It used to be said that there were no bad soldiers, only bad officers, but the managers were punch drunk. The balance of power was tilted against them, and industrial disputes and wage negotiations diverted them from the business of managing. Some had abdicated. In the old industrial areas many firms survived on government support and workers on job creation schemes. Small wonder that some managers hesitated before voting for the free but cold world offered by Margaret Thatcher. It was time for a change, but he was not at all certain that the government could achieve its first objective of encouraging the creation of wealth.

Thorneycroft paused, his slow eyes fixed on the panorama of chimney pots outside the window. We had reached a turning point in the conversation, and after talking to other Tory politicians I guessed what he was about to say. I was to be told in some oblique fashion that Thatcher was not the Iron Lady, Attila the Hen, or She, Who Must Be Obeyed.

He allowed that Thatcher had weaknesses, which he did not enumerate, but she had many gifts: determination, instinct, passion and that quality of inconsistency shared by all great people. She knew that the Tories' greatest strength was that they were not a party of dogma, that they were pragmatists. Basically, she was a good housewife whose instincts told her that the country could not go on spending more than it earned. Hence the need to create wealth if the social services were to be maintained. It would not be easy. Cutting taxes and holding down public expenditure would not be enough.

Central Office had reviewed all the possibilities since her elevation to the leadership, from incomes policy to mechanics of monetarism, and had decided that neither extreme could work because of union opposition. The Tories had subdued the bishops and the landlords in the past, and if necessary – he hesitated briefly and then went on – they would subdue militant trade unionists. Nevertheless, Thatcher had recognized that a strict monetarist policy would be too damaging.

Other Tories, as already indicated, had also suggested that Thatcher was not an implacable ideologue. One man who was to join her Cabinet was convinced, or perhaps he was trying to convince himself, that although she could be aggressive and extremist if given the chance, the members of the Shadow Cabinet were different from the last Tory Cabinet. Heath had had no one to stand up to him, but she would have men such as Whitelaw, Carrington, Pym and Prior who were strong enough to reason with her.

He was not entirely persuasive if only because Whitelaw, Carrington, Pym and Prior had served in the Heath Cabinet, and I concluded that they had not persuaded themselves.

They were still apprehensive about her monetarist ideas and her determination to restrain public spending as well as her attitude to the trade unions. Most of them had been cast in the Macmillan mould, and they remembered Saltley, Heath's defeat and the more recent winter of discontent. Some of them were worried about the possibility of increased violence, and were not convinced that legislation or the police could stop well-organized flying pickets. The certainty that unemployment would get worse before it got better was also worrying. Above all, they were afraid of another violent swing of the pendulum, from the right to a point well beyond left of centre.

In other words, the Tory leadership was divided; not as much as Labour, but the semi-isolation of Thatcher became clear when she formed her first Cabinet. Of the twenty-two members only four – Sir Keith Joseph, John Nott, Angus Maude and John Biffen – shared her views of how to run the economy, and they did not necessarily share her views of how to run the country. She was very vulnerable.

SEVEN

There Was Once Poetry in Machines

With his red face and blue eyes, Jim Prior looked every inch the farmer when we walked round his Suffolk farm one splendid summer morning. We had dined well the night before but he radiated rude health as we inspected the beef cattle and discussed the latest method of drilling wheat. Afterwards we sat in the sun and drank a large jug of Buck's Fizz, which was fizzier than usual because a generous hand had poured the champagne. It was very pleasant, but Prior was not the rich man playing the part of gentleman farmer. He had read estate management at Cambridge, and after coming down had managed the farm of a Tory MP. That helped to explain his eventual entry into politics by way of the National Farmers' Union and the local constituency party, but his wellies had remained firmly on the ground. He bought his 400-acre farm with a loan, and farmed it with only one man even when he went to Westminster. It was highly mechanized and efficiently run.

Prior was elected to Parliament as the Member for Lowestoft in 1959 and made his mark as Parliamentary Private Secretary to Edward Heath, who was leader of the party. He was appointed Minister of Agriculture, Food and Fisheries when the Tories returned to power in 1970, and was Lord President of the Council and Leader of the House of Commons when they were defeated four years later. No doubt his friendship with Heath helped to explain the fairly rapid promotion, but his earthy common sense was appreciated on both sides of the House and his affability made him a favourite in the Smoking Room. He was the model for the hero in Simon Raven's political novels.

His shrewdness and courage equipped him for high if not the highest office. Even his friends doubted that he would ever become Prime Minister because he was thought to lack the ruthlessness that carries men to the top. Nevertheless they regretted that he first went to Ag. and Fish and not the Ministry of Employment where his down-to-earth qualities might have helped to avoid the misunderstandings which led to the miners' strike and the downfall of the Tory government. He finally made it to Employment in 1979 after shadowing the post during the years of opposition.

Even then Prior's appointment was something of a surprise because he did not seem to be the man to carry out Mrs. Thatcher's trade union policy, and during the election campaign was said not to be confident of getting the job. Thatcher was thought to be too suspicious of his trade union friendships and his instinct for conciliation, but he had tempered the radicalism of Keith Joseph when they had served together in her Shadow Cabinet. He had also persuaded Thatcher to soften the section on labour legislation in the party manifesto, and everybody agreed that he was the best Tory Employment Minister available.

Prior was certainly closer to the unions than any of his Cabinet colleagues. He liked people, whatever their party label, occupation or class. His father had been a Norwich solicitor, but he had the gregariousness of ordinary working class folk. He did not have the capacity for absorbing the vast quantities of liquor, which perhaps most separates the older generation of the trade union movement from their juniors. He preferred wine, but nursing his beer he had sat through many a long, loquacious and boozy evening with union leaders, and thought he knew them well. A few had confessed into their pint pots that restrictive practices and industrial indiscipline were impoverishing their members, that there had to be a better way of running unions and the country. This had persuaded him that many of them would welcome some measure of labour legislation, but he was convinced that legalistic solutions alone would not work. Moreover, he recognized that the employers were as much to blame as the unions for Britain's economic decline.

He had learned a great deal from the consequences of Heath's Industrial Relations Act. It had provided employers with the opportunity to stand up to the unions, and they had failed to use it. This had convinced him that they wanted to avoid trouble whatever the cost. They wanted the government to fight their battles, but this could not be done. Sir Hector Laing, the chairman of United Biscuits, afterwards showed what had to be done when he sought an injunction against secondary picketing in 1979, but very few other employers had had the guts. They had been subdued by the unions.

Many of them had in fact taken Confucius's advice on rape. They had accepted the inevitable, and while not particularly enjoying it life became a little less harrowing. Their longing for a little peace and quiet was understandable. In some industries, notably car manufacture and newspaper publishing, they could spend about two-thirds of their time negotiating with unions, and

121

they took the easy way out. Even in a growth industry such as North Sea oil managers had to devote at least a quarter of their time to industrial relations. Employers generally paid wage increases above the costs of capital and costs of living, and accepted over-manning and out-dated work practices. Arguably there was no alternative other than going out of business, although imminent bankruptcy had been known to persuade some unions to reduce their demands. Alas, there was a third alternative, state subsidy. The government was always prepared to rescue lame ducks if bankruptcy and loss of jobs were politically damaging, and they joined the queue of supplicants.

One economist, Graham Hutton, said that British man-agements were spineless, apathetic, ignorant, complacent, and cushioned by government; but union rape was of course only the most recent development which had made four out of five British companies less efficient than those in other industrial democracies. If Prior had read history instead of estate management at Cambridge he would have known that British industry generally had been cushioned by governments long before the rise of militant trade unionism. Empire trade was the obvious example.

Not at first of course. Captain Hippon was on his own when he established the first British trading post in India, at Masulipatam in 1610. He and other merchant adventurers who followed made enormous profits which helped to fund the industrial revolution. The casualty rate was high; the graves of those who died from disease or war can still be found from Karachi to Hongkong, but it was the courage and initiative of individuals at home and abroad which made Britain the world's leading trading nation. The flag continued to follow trade until Clive's victory at Plassey transformed the East India Company into a ruling power on the sub-continent. Arguably that was when the rot set in. Thereafter trade tended to follow the flag, and traders gradually became camp followers as imperial expansion created protected markets.

This dependence was eventually formalized at Ottawa in 1932 when imperial preferences were negotiated between Britain and the dominions. No doubt it seemed to make sense at the time. World trade was still depressed and the system provided guaranteed markets for dominion and colonial primary products as well as British manufactures, but preferential treatment further blunted the competitive spirit of British businessmen. They stopped trying harder despite increasing competition from the United States and Germany, and the directors and managers of the larger companies assumed the life style of the landed gentry.

The process of gentrification had begun with the nabobs, the successful traders who returned from India laden with loot and profits and built themselves large country houses. The literature of the times shows that they were regarded as upstarts and figures of fun, but they were absorbed into the higher strata of society within a couple of generations. A similar process was evident abroad, especially in India where it had all begun. The boxwallahs, as they were known, had a pecking order of their own similar to that of the Indian Civil Service and the armed forces. Cheap servants and low taxation gave them illusions of grandeur. They were largely responsible for maintaining the colour bar in clubs long after the ICS and the armed forces had accepted Indian-born officials and officers as equals, and they reinforced the British class system when they retired.

The home-grown boxwallahs also had their illusions of grandeur, especially in London. In the lovely halls of the City livery companies they wore medieval garments often trimmed with fur and drank wines that would have impressed a Rothschild. At the Mansion House pikemen in Cromwellian uniform provided a guard of honour and they went into dinner to the beat of a drum. At the Lord Mayor's banquet in the Guildhall the Prime Minister of the day addressed these alleged captains of industry and slowly disappeared behind their clouds of cigar smoke while Britain continued to slide down the drain.

They had come a long way since that landing at Masulipatam and Tocqueville's Birmingham. The country had paid another heavy price for imperialism, and was still paying it long after the end of empire. The bad old habits were passed on to the next generation who continued to live in a semi-closed world of executive dining rooms, exclusive golf clubs and company cars. They were not necessarily second-raters protected and advanced because they went to the right schools. Many were shrewd men capable of running successful companies when they were allowed to do so, but the competitive edge of the majority had been blunted by imperial preferences, social circumstance and finally trade union militancy.

As a result, after the second world war Britain dropped from second to twentieth place in the league of economic powers. It ceased being the workshop of the world and became an importing nation. In 1979 the volume of imports of manufactured goods increased by 18 per cent, nearly five times the growth of exports. The import of foreign cars alone cost more than £2,600 million, or more than the profits from North Sea oil. The machine tool industry was on its last legs, temporarily propped up by the National Enterprise Board. We were opting out of manufacturing, and de-industrialization continued.

No less alarming was the reluctance of young people to seek a career in manufacturing, because it could lead eventually to the complete de-industrialization of Britain. Entrants were so few that engineering schools could not survive without foreign students. When the Thatcher government increased charges for foreign students one complaint was that the engineering schools would collapse without them. Nobody seemed to realize the significance of this, nevertheless to some extent the reluctance of British students to go into engineering was understandable. The promotion prospects for engineering students were less bright than for those who went into the management or sales side of industry or the administrative grade of the Civil Service. Less tangible but no less influential was the social ambience. The pretentions of the bosses permeated the next layers of the social pyramid, and even infected graduates of polytechnics. The old northern saying, where there is muck there is brass, repelled rather than attracted. The growth of service industries offered them alternative and pleasanter opportunities in office blocks or trading estates in the Southeast.

It is possible to see this as a further development in the process of gentrification, which began with the trickle of returning nabobs from India in the seventeenth and eighteenth centuries. By the late twentieth century it was apparently irreversible at every level of society, including ordinary families who had earlier apprenticed their sons to a good trade.

The educational system was partly responsible. For the best possible reasons, to provide equal opportunity and nurture equality, the assumption of post-war liberal educators was that most youngsters wanted to get to Oxbridge or at second best the redbrick and white-tile universities. They appeared to be unaware of the obvious; that an industrial country could not be manned by academics and that over the centuries many people had found, and still find, greater satisfaction in being craftsmen. I was reminded of this when reading for the third or fourth time A. G. Macdonell's *England, Their England*. The author was that rare Scotsman who genuinely liked the English, and while the book pokes fun at us Sassenachs the gentle humour reveals more of the island race than any heavy academic tome. The usual English stereotypes are examined and dismissed with a friendly pat on the head, but towards the end of the book emerges a man whom he clearly admired. He is William Rhodes, an engineer from Yorkshire, who had spent much of his life inventing and fabricating machines and the remainder teaching the natives of almost every member nation of the United Nations how to operate them. He is the prototype British engineer of the old school.

Rhodes speaks for his fellow craftsmen aboard a dirty Polish tramp whose engines he had just repaired. Holding out his two great thin hands, he says with perfect simplicity, 'I can make any machine in the world with these two. I'm a craftsman, lad, as good as any in the North Country. And it isn't only that . . . There's poetry in machines. You'll maybe not understand. But that's how I see it. Some folks like books and music and poems, but I get all of that out of machines. I take a lot of steel and I put it into different shapes, and it works. It works. D'you see? It works as true as a hair to the thousandth part of an inch just as I made it and meant it. I'll go on making machines till my dying day, even if it's only toy engines for grandchildren.'

Too romantic? Perhaps, but not so many years ago when I wandered about the world on an expense account I met many such as William Rhodes. They built bridges, harbours and factories, as earlier they had built railways in every continent. They had a pride of craft comparable with a soldier's pride of regiment. Their pride was shared by men working on the shop floor at home, as I was reminded recently by Reg Birch, the Maoist trade union leader. When still an engineering apprentice he woke very early one Sunday morning remembering that he had incorrectly set a machine, and the shame drove him back to the factory. He broke in like a burglar, re-set the machine and was back in bed before his mother got up to cook breakfast.

Those liberal educators knew little or nothing about the pride of craftsmanship which once gave men immense dignity, but possibly they were to be forgiven because as a country we have had little respect for the source of our wealth. We launched the industrial revolution but left it to the Germans and Americans to establish technical high schools, agricultural and mechanical colleges, institutes of technology and business schools. The engineers were rarely rewarded and recognized.

There are not so many of them now. One of William Rhodes's sons became a schoolmaster, the other a parson, and the sons of today's engineers and craftsmen are also looking elsewhere for advancement. Belatedly they are now being encouraged by the government to enter engineering and trade schools, but the ethos of the country does not encourage them. Apart from social attitudes, those on the shop floor also feel threatened as their differentials are squeezed by trade union demands for the unskilled. The government, bosses and unions have only themselves to blame for the de-industrialization of Britain.

*

Britain still has some merchant adventurers, efficient companies and good craftsmen. Sir Freddie Laker, Marks and Spencer and Rolls Royce engineers are obvious examples. It also has some successful industries. The City of London, for instance, although one well-dressed City gent objected to the suggestion that he was engaged in industry. A few critics also said that success had been achieved at a price, of which more later, but there was general agreement that the City was a typical but successful British institution.

Crowded into little more than one square mile, many of its office blocks are built on the old Roman wall and other historical remains. As Denis Brogan said, 'Business goes on in buildings whose foundations and parts of whose walls go back to the days of Hadrian, when London was the great western city of the Empire that stretched to the Tigris, the Sahara and the Upper Nile. But it would be rash to do business with the people using these buildings on the assumption that their command of arithmetical method was no better than that of their Roman predecessors. For hundreds of years the smartest businessmen in the world have been coming in to the City of London from Amsterdam and Paris and Frankfurt and Genoa and Smyrna and Boston, and the survival of Roman and medieval foundations in the City has not prevented it from being the successor of Carthage and Venice.'*

Brogan was writing mainly for an American readership, and no doubt many of them wanted to be reassured that the junior partner of the special relationship could recover after the war and eventual loss of empire. There was small reason to believe that the City would when peace came. It had no capital resources for lending abroad except in the sterling area, inactive markets, a currency that was hardly stable, massive sterling debts and a suspicious Labour government. Its old predominance of the global market in invisibles – trade in services and returns on investment rather than in goods – was threatened by Zurich and New York.

Zurich had emerged from the war backed by a thriving economy, the advantages of neutrality, banking secrecy and a strong currency. In the popular imagination the gnomes of Zurich, as its City men were described by Harold Wilson, were seen to be a sinister cabal manipulating the markets to the detriment of Britain. New York commanded the strongest international currency and belonged to the richest country in the world; while the City had to scour the world for business, its once well-tailored representatives threadbare, its coffers empty.

The outlook was bleak, but within fifteen years the City had re-emerged in a dominant position and flourished despite the com-

* *The English People*. Hamish Hamilton, London, 1942.

petition of the new financial centres. By the late seventies the City earned no less than £2,300 millions in foreign income a year. Its earnings had in fact increased over five times in a decade, and accounted for over a third of the country's invisible earnings.*

The City had reasserted its lead in part because it was efficient and modern under the medieval guise. In 1979, according to Clarke, it had the largest international turnover in insurance, and its banks had many more foreign branches than any foreign rival. It rivalled Zurich in gold transactions, and claimed the largest share of the Eurocurrency market. Once again, it attracted smart businessmen from all over the world, and eventually had more foreign banks than any other city. Its turnover in foreign exchange was bigger than New York's. The Baltic Exchange undertook well over half of the world's shipping freights, and several of its commodity markets had the biggest world turnover in spot transactions. The London Stock Exchange had the largest listing of foreign securities, and its turnover was bigger than the other European exchanges put together.

There were several reasons why the City flourished while other traditional industries such as shipbuilding were beaten by foreign competitors. Again, the heavy hand of trade unionism was absent, and government regulations were remarkably few. Despite the occasional surviving bowler hat and rolled umbrella, the old piratical spirit was also still in evidence. Certainly it had not been stifled by Empire trade. Instead, the City was one sector of British industry that still benefited from the imperial period in a very real way. The Union Jack had been lowered for the last time all over the world, the troops and governors had departed to Aldershot and Cheltenham, but the banks, insurance offices and shipping agents remained. This world-wide network, and the City's own expertise, were the foundations of the City's post-war success.

Another reason was that the City attracted many shrewd and clever men because the potential rewards were so high. Among them were bright working-class boys such as Jim Slater and Peter Walker, but many more came from the upper strata of the social pyramid if only because there was no more congenial way of making lots of money. They tended to be politically and socially influential, in part because of their background but also because the City had long worked closely with government. They had access to successive Chancellors to an extent rarely available to mere producers of wealth, and used it to their own advantage.

Theirs was a remarkable success by any standard, but a heavy price was paid. They did not necessarily help British industry

* *Inside the City* by William M. Clarke. Allen and Unwin, 1979

because their markets were largely international. Indeed, Clarke said that the City was criticized for letting down British industry, that it was accused of deliberately speculating against the pound and exporting hard-earned British savings. High interest rates also attracted unwanted hot money from abroad, thereby adding to the instability of the whole economy. Harold Lever was a more forthright critic.

Lever was once said to be capitalism's fifth column in the Labour party, and he was well equipped for the part. He was a self-made millionaire, whose second marriage made him a multi-millionaire, and after a number of ministerial appointments he became Harold Wilson's economic and financial adviser with a seat in the Cabinet.

We met in his duplex apartment in Eaton Square, which looked as if it had been furnished for an oil sheikh and not for the son of an immigrant Orthodox Jewish family. He was not born poor, he went to Manchester Grammar School and read law at Manchester University, but he was born in the radical tradition of British politics and never veered from it despite his increasing wealth and bourgeois habits. (The calf-bound volumes in his apartment looked unread but he was a devoted theatre- and opera-goer.) He was also a genuinely funny man with a comedian's face more often than not creased by a grin even after a stroke left him with useless arm and gammy leg.

Lever was one of the few Labour ministers who understood the City. He was fascinated by macro-economics, and was capable of pitting his judgement and financial flair against the Treasury knights, Keynesian to a man, and prejudices of ministerial colleagues. He saved them from themselves on more than one occasion, and was instrumental in rescuing the pound in 1976 by helping to put together the international package that placed the government's spending under the firm curbs of the International Monetary Fund in return for support of the pound.

The Treasury knights and some people in the City tended to sneer. The unasked question, at least in public, was what did this Manchester Jewish financier know about economics. The sneer was almost certainly not anti-Semitic but rather reflected the snobbery of top civil servants and City people. Well, he had his weaknesses, but he understood world trade and its financing. He also knew that Keynesian economics had had its day, and was opposed to large-scale deficit spending. He also saw capitalism as a tool for social democracy, which was why he had a low opinion of the City.

When we met in Eaton Square surrounded by those calf-bound books and representational furniture, Lever said that the City, for all its invisible earnings, had done as much damage to the country as had the trade union movement's hostility to management. Long after we had lost the Empire, the City was allowed to regard the pound and sterling balances as our claim to great power status. It persuaded successive governments to maintain sterling as a reserve currency for years after it had lost ground to stronger currencies such as the Swiss franc, the Deutschmark and the Japanese yen.

High finance was treated like a sacred thing, and the City as high priests. It was nonsense, enjoyable nonsense if you could afford it, but it had a terrible effect upon the economy. It had led to the stop-go policies which had devastated British industry as had high interest rates. These quite dreadful consequences had been recognized at the time, they could hardly be avoided unless you stopped reading newspapers and listening to the radio, but successive Chancellors had been persuaded to sacrifice British industry to maintain sterling as a reserve currency. Lever allowed that the City and the trade unions were not entirely to blame. Governments all over the world intervened in their economies, if none so disastrously as Whitehall. The bosses, unlike their continental counterparts, were also victims of the usual class nonsense and could not comprehend that making money was a fine and honourable bourgeois pursuit – especially when it enabled them to enjoy culture.

I pondered Lever's remark afterwards because he was the first during the course of this enquiry to use the word bourgeois in a non-pejorative sense. The far left had regarded the bourgeoisie as enemies of the people, and the culturally arrogant of both parties had confused them with Poujadists. That had not been my experience during the years spent in western Europe as a foreign correspondent, although it had taken me some time to appreciate that upper- or middle-class was a poor translation of bourgeoisie. Such terminology was inadequate in societies without an hereditary class, and I turned once again to the *Fontana Dictionary of Modern Thought* for a better definition.

'Since the 19th century . . . the bourgeoisie was regarded as open, adventurous, and revolutionary; thus Marx, in the *Communist Manifesto*, writes: "The bourgeoisie, historically, has played a most revolutionary part . . . The bourgeoisie cannot exist without constantly revolutionizing the instruments of production . . . and with them the whole relations of society." The political revolutions effected by the bourgeoisie, particularly the French Revolution, ended privileges based on birth, and stressed individualism and achievement as the criteria of place and position in society . . .'

A case for the bourgeoisie was well put by William Pfaff when he compared the elites of Britain and France.* In Britain, he wrote, 'It has been an elite of honourable service as well as privilege, willing to lead and die in Britain's wars, ambitious for the country and doing well for it, on the whole, and even saving it on occasion (it is not, perhaps, too much to say that of 1940), but also doing well from it and, by its hereditary character and claim to privilege, serving as a cause of bitterness and alienation – perpetuating Britain's divisions, limiting its possibilities. This has been the most enduring aristocracy in Europe, strong because it is, properly speaking, a meritocratic governing class assimilated to an aristocracy and to the values of that aristocracy. Those values are essentially agricultural, anti-industrial, anti-capitalist; the social ideal is the landowning gentleman.'

Pfaff went on to say that the British majority seemed to want the hereditary class to survive, but a sizeable part of the public simply refused to concede legitimacy to the leadership of a hereditary social class. The honours system was supposed to be a good, pragmatic compromise of tradition with merit, but it had 'not cured the tension between classes and the social resentment that is so marked in Britain and that continues to obstruct its economic and industrial adaptation to the challenge of its neighbours.'

A comparison with France, Pfaff continued, was illuminating because the French historical inheritance was much more narrowly monarchical, absolutist and aristocratic than the British. France today might be said to have an aristocratic government, with an elected monarch, and in certain respects it was an authoritarian government. But the aristocracy had been laicized. This lay aristocracy, originally an elite of the Civil Service and formed in a group of special schools, the *grandes écoles*, now managed a significant part of private as well as state enterprise and held a leading position in the country's political life, including the parties of the opposition. Entrance to this elite was by examination open to all. It was egalitarian, and an elite so recruited was perceived to be legitimate. 'Legitimacy is the crucial element. With legitimacy, the French elite, unlike the British, unifies rather than divides.'

I am not commending the French system, despite my Gallic grandfather. In any case, before imperialism and gentrification perverted them, Victorian Liberals, not the party but its middle-class members, promised a better society. They were the natural leaders of the then emerging new Britain, liberated not so much by coal and iron as the apparently boundless opportunities they promised. In a recent book about their lives and times†, Ian

* The *New Yorker*, January 14, 1980
† *The Optimists*, Faber, 1980

Bradley said that Britain then came nearest in its history to banishing vested interest and class from determining its politics and instead establishing the rule of ideas and principles.

Bright understood this when he attacked the Tories in 1866. 'If a class has failed, let us try the nation.' He meant of course the new and enlightened middle class, the burgeoning bourgeoisie. The word was French, meaning a member of a free city, a burgher if you like who was neither a peasant or a lord. A German, Karl Marx, gave it a new meaning, but the example was British and they expressed the ambitions of many working class folk. They were largely motivated by their nonconformist conscience, very much a British phenomenon, and the desire for progress, self-determination and self-improvement. They could have broken down class barriers and united the new Britain.

They failed because Victoria was on the throne, the empire beckoned, and, as has happened so often in British history, they were before their time. Their descendants could have made a go of it after the second world war, but . . . Lever did not enlarge upon his concept of the bourgeoisie. Perhaps because of his Talmudic training – his grandfather had singled him out for instruction in the body of Jewish law and legend – he supposed that we would never solve the mysteries of life. He suggested that the British were not made for modern industrial life. 'You have to be as greedy as the French, as docile as the Germans, and as ant-like as the Japanese to accept the disciplines of the modern technological world. Probably the British are too bloody-minded and libertarian.'

· This could be part of the ethos, a more interesting part than the guilt complex of the middle class, the wet socialism of Fabianism and the Oxbridge disdain of the outside world. Oxbridge, he added, and his contempt appeared to cover its graduates in politics, the Civil Service and the private sector, were prepared to accept the national decline gracefully. Because of their arrogance, they were sublimely unaware of the tough-mindedness of the provincial British.

*

I first met Lord Sieff in Tel Aviv when I was covering the 1948 Arab-Israel war and he was serving as a volunteer in the Israel army with the *nom de guerre* of Wolff. The badges of rank had been removed from the blouse of his battledress, but he looked every inch the British officer and gentleman. When we next met in 1980, soon after his ennoblement, he looked not so much the British lord as the laicized aristocrat Pfaff wrote about in his appreciation of the bourgeoisie.

Probably he would not have become chairman of Marks and Spencer Ltd., one of Britain's most successful companies, if he had not been the son of his father, but equally there was little doubt that he had also got to the top because he was intelligent and shrewd. Another product of the Manchester Grammar School – which he left for St Paul's when the family moved to London – he matriculated when he was fourteen and later won the Hambro Award, Businessman of the Year in 1977.

Sieff was wearing a M & S suit, which had sold for £65 the previous year, when we met at the company's headquarters in Baker Street, just up the road from where Sherlock Holmes used to live. He had the easy manner of the truly classless, and clearly saw the pursuit of profit as a fine and honourable profession. In so doing he had helped to expand the company, which had its small beginnings on a market stall in Leeds, into a giant with 250 stores and a world-wide reputation for good products. It also took good care of its 43,000 employees and had been rewarded with loyal service and decades of strike-free expansion.

He believed in the capitalist and market economy systems because they had raised living standards higher than any other system while maintaining individual freedom. He refused to believe that Britain did not have the will to overcome its economic and social problems, and argued that what was lacking was leadership and a care for people's needs and an understanding of their aspirations. The main problem was not the lack of investment, energy, new technologies or inflation, but how to develop a cooperative relationship in all spheres of human endeavour. People expected better living standards and quality of life because standards of education had improved immensely over the years. Most of them wanted to be kept informed of developments affecting them, they appreciated their advice had been sought and this emphasized the importance of establishing good human relations in industry. Such relations could not be imposed by government; they could only develop organically within each organization.

Loyalty was an important factor in Sieff's and the company's philosophy; loyalty to employees, suppliers, customers, communities in which the stores operated and to the country. Sieff described it as moral obligation and went on to suggest that what was good for Britain was good for M & S. He recalled without rancour that after his return from the Israel war a Special Branch officer asked him to surrender his passport. Being a reserve officer at the time, he had apparently offended some regulation by serving in a foreign army. The matter was straightened out after Sieff had said that he knew four British officers who had served with the Arab Legion, but the Special Branch man could not have known much about the man or company.

In 1980, despite the flood of imports, 93 percent of M & S's products were still made in Britain. This was the company's policy but was not always easy to implement; while Britain still made fine woollens other countries made better or cheaper cottons and corduroy. But by working closely with suppliers the company had helped to improve the local product and achieve competitive prices. Thirty of the suppliers had traded with the company for 40 years, another 125 for more than 30 years and one supplier for nearly a century. This loyal association had guaranteed long production runs for suppliers, who in turn had accepted the high standards required.

Sieff said that it had been very difficult at times. For instance, a Japanese manufacturer had recently offered the company a fabric at half the price of their own supplier. It was a reputable firm and the fabric was excellent, but they had stayed with the British supplier after discussing ways of reducing production costs. The supplier would have been bankrupted otherwise, about 1,000 workers would have lost their jobs, and Britain and M & S would eventually have suffered.

There can be few other British firms with a similar loyalty or sense of moral obligation, and fewer have had better human relations with its workers. Sieff said that human relations were essential in industry. It was a choice of human or industrial relations, cooperation or confrontation. There was no half-way house.

Human relations, Sieff said, had to start with the board respecting the individual. Directors had to understand that a right and just personnel policy was essential for success, that it had to be known to all employees and seen to be honoured. It must include a progressive wage policy which would share the prosperity of the company with employees and ensure their well-being in every possible way. It required substantial physical and mental effort, and a great deal of money. Apart from higher wages, it had cost the company £35 million in 1979. It might seem mad, but not totally mad when you looked at the bottom line of the balance sheet.

As with many old-established British companies, in the early years his grandfather had known every employee, most of them by name. This became impossible as the company grew, and a personnel department was set up whose head, a very senior director, had a staff of 900 of whom 700 worked in the stores. Each looked after between 50 and 75 people. They were line managers and had other tasks, but their prime responsibility was the well-being and progress of their people. They had to know them personally, and do whatever was necessary to ensure their well-being.

Establishing good human relations was a long process. M & S launched its personnel policy in 1929, during the depression when there were few welfare services. Every store was given a decent staff restaurant, and a morning snack, a good dinner and afternoon tea cost six old pennies a day. That price was held until 1978 when it went up to 50 new pence a week. The company had also concerned itself with the health of the work force since 1933, and despite the National Health Service there was still much scope for individual medical care. The medical department supervised the store doctors and dentists who were always available for consultation and nine out of ten of the staff attended. The system of testing for cervical and breast cancer had saved a number of lives and revealed other ailments which the person concerned thought could not be cured or did not bother about. Chiropodists and hairdressers were also available.

The non-contributory pension scheme cost about £20 million a year. Employees retired at 60 and their pension was the equivalent of two-thirds of their pay after 33 years of service – the highest allowed by the Revenue. In the event of death, the wife or nearest dependent was paid the equivalent of three years' salary tax free. Pensioners were looked after until their dying day. They were attached to the store nearest their homes and received all medical services free and little services such as free hairdressing for the women. Under a profit-sharing scheme about 18,000 employees had also become shareholders. The result, Sieff said, was a profitable and reasonably efficient business with a loyal staff taking pride in their work. The vast majority responded. They happily accepted the benefits and the obligations. Absenteeism was minimal even during the most dreadful winters.

Such services were important, but it was essential for the board to remain in constant touch with the labour force. M & S directors were required to visit stores as often as possible. They were expected to talk to all the supervisors and listen to what employees had to say. He had learned a great deal from such visits. It was a two-way traffic. People wanted to be liked and respected, and had something to offer. They also wanted to be kept informed about the company, its progress, future plans and problems. In his experience practically nothing was absolutely confidential, and when employees knew what was going on, or what was likely to happen, there were no shocks when problems did arise.

I suggested that it was easy for Marks and Spencer because the work force was not unionized and the vast majority were women. Sieff disagreed. It made no difference when good human relations nurtured loyalty and trust on both sides. United Biscuits operated many factories in this country with about 20,000 factory employees. About half of them were men, and all the factories were completely unionized. The company was successful because it had deliberately set out to involve its people in matters concerning them, and most had behaved responsibly. Full disclosure of the company's results was also made to the unions.

As Jim Prior had recalled earlier, Sir Hector Laing, the chairman of United Biscuits, had successfully sought an injunction against secondary picketing during the road haulage strike, but he was not a union basher. He only wanted to run his company according to certain rules agreed to by management and unions. At the time of the road haulage strike he was trying to persuade his employees to negotiate a contract based on added value; that is the difference between what the company was paid for its products and the cost of materials and services. Laing guaranteed the work force 70 percent if they agreed that at least 15 percent must be allocated to re-investment to keep the company competitive. He also guaranteed job security: five years' guaranteed employment after three years and employment until retirement after ten.

Sieff obviously admired Laing because they shared the same view about human relations and personal leadership in industry, and he said that British Leyland would not have gone bankrupt if Lord Stokes had pursued a similar policy. BL was a terrible example of a company whose failure was due largely to its failure to develop a spirit of cooperation between management and employees. The original Morris management, under Lord Nuffield, had cared for its people and relations were good. The Austin management did not, and when the two companies were merged to become the British Motor Corporation in 1952, the new company did badly because of the poor relationship between managers and men.

Leyland, a small but successful company, was then persuaded by the Labour government in the sixties to merge with BMC and form British Leyland. Sieff said it was ridiculous for a profitable sprat to swallow an unprofitable whale. Lord Stokes, the new chairman, came to see him and said that he had a hell of a problem because he had to close down twenty plants if the new company was to prosper. Sieff advised him to develop a decent personnel policy before he did anything, but Stokes said he did not have the time. Things went from bad to worse, a good policy was eventually drafted but the company went broke before it could be implemented.

This was typical of firms growing too quickly, often by mergers and takeovers. The well-established human relations of the

135

original firm were often overwhelmed by the very size of the new undertaking. Big was not necessarily beautiful. Sometimes the bad practices of one of the merged firms became the standard for all, and the militants were given the opportunity to create trouble. They could use every genuine grievance, and create a few of their own, to subvert our socio-economic system into class warfare between 'us and them'. Nevertheless, it must always be remembered that communist trade union leaders could only take advantage of weak or bad management. They were not dangerous when companies nurtured good human relations.

*

The Confederation of British Industry is often regarded as the bosses' union, and the many Rolls Royce cars which clog Tothill Street when its council meets certainly gives that impression. It represents more than 13,000 companies and some 200 commercial, employer and trade associations. Many member companies are small, employing less than 50 workers, but most of the country's top 1,000 companies are affiliated. Together they employ about 12 million people, approximately the strength of the trade union movement, but the CBI does not have the power or influence of the TUC.

The Confederation is close to the Conservative party, but is not part of it organizationally as the trade unions are part of the Labour party. It has no bloc votes to turn the Tories in the direction it might want them to move, and most of the businessmen it represents are impatient with politics. Consequently the CBI does not have the political influence of the TUC. It was not a component of the quasi-corporate state which was developing before Mrs. Thatcher came to power. Sir John Methven, the late director general, would not have had it otherwise although he wanted to provide some balance to the TUC.

When we met in his office one evening, a few months before his death, he proved to be an amiable man with large ears and an india-rubber face which smiled easily. He was soft spoken and philosophical, and reminded me of Len Murray whom he liked and respected. Methven also opened a bottle of white wine as we talked in his office at the end of the working day. Despite the late hour, the conversation was interrupted by phone calls as at Congress House, and again like Murray he seemed willing to talk for the rest of the evening.

Other comparisons could be made, but Methven, the son of a Newcastle businessman, had begun his working life as a solicitor with the Birmingham Corporation. He transferred to Imperial

Chemical Industries because he needed more money to educate his three children, and became deputy chairman of the Mond division. He sat on the Monopolies and Bullock Commissions, and then left ICI with a cut in salary to become director-general of the Office of Fair Trading. He was a notable success at OFT in part because he was impatient with bureaucratic formality and proved to be a successful communicator. He joined the CBI because he thought that the case for private enterprise was going by default.

Methven did not believe that Britain was going down the drain. We were the only great imperial power which had lost an empire without internal political and social convulsions. This surely meant that we had inner strengths and were capable of achieving much by voluntary and democratic means. His work at OFT had persuaded him that a great deal could be done by persuasion because on the whole we were a reasonable people. Nevertheless, without an empire we were like a man and wife whose children had grown up and gone, and had then discovered that only the children had kept them together. We were also an easy-going people who preferred not to face facts, which had pluses and minuses.

One of the main faults was the absence of a market philosophy. He believed strongly in the market economy. It had improved living standards, and had made the welfare state possible. It was a greater power for good than any political philosophy, but as represented in Britain it looked inhuman and uncaring. The socalled progressive forces, including the Socialist Workers party, seemed caring although they had little to offer except inhibiting government regulations and the corporate state. The Labour party and the trade unions also looked caring, but were bankrupt of ideas. In the absence of a market philosophy, as understood and accepted in other industrial democracies, Britain had been moving towards a corporate state. This was the weakness of Len Murray's tripartitism. Methven added that he had to be careful in organizing industry to balance the trade unions not to turn it into a component of the corporate state. That had to be avoided, the country could only recover and flourish with a market economy.

The CBI did in fact begin to resemble the TUC under Methven's direction. He organized the first annual CBI conference in order to acquire visible parity with the TUC. The hope was that in future television and Fleet Street would have to devote as much time and space to the CBI conference as it had always given to the political parties and the TUC. A fund to help strike-bound companies was also proposed. The normal reaction if a company was struck, and Methven supposed it was the natural reaction in a market economy, was for competitors to see the strike as an opportunity to pinch customers or to bring pressure to bear for a settlement whatever the cost. But member companies had to recognize how inter-dependent they were, and perhaps provide mutual financial support for each other in the event of major disputes.

Methven said that Britain was still doing some things remarkably well; banking, insurance, retailing and tourism were obvious examples. Only manufacturing and engineering had fared badly, and strikes and restrictive practices were not entirely to blame. The prime responsibility for improving productivity rested with management at all levels, and unfortunately managers who organized production did not enjoy a high status in Britain. They were on average less qualified, given less authority and were less well paid than their opposite numbers in other industrial democracies. As a consequence production had attracted fewer able recruits in Britain than in West Germany and France, although this was changing. Nor was over-manning confined to the shop floor. British firms tended to have larger managerial and administrative staffs than other EEC companies.

Methven was confident that productivity could be improved if only the attitudes of managers and trade union leaders could be changed, but another problem was government intervention. He supposed it was inevitable in a declining society, but with the best of intentions it had had disastrous results.

I had heard this complaint frequently during the course of my enquiry, in trade union offices as well as in boardrooms, on the left as well as the right. It was well documented. *The Economist*, in one of its school briefs, said that almost every form of intervention and control had been tried, from carrot to stick, to increase the efficiency of Britain's ailing industry. One major criticism was that with so much chopping and changing no policy had had a chance to succeed before it had been replaced by the next. Keith Richardson had written in *The Sunday Times*, 'If you actually sat down and tried to draw up a national plan for throwing a modern industrial society on its beam ends you could hardly have done better than this combination of less-than-three-percent growth, violent zig-zags of economic policy every two years (and) drastic shifts in the relationship between government and industry.'

The zig-zags were of course closely related to changes of government referred to earlier in this book. A report published by the Hansard Society for Parliamentary Government* gave this quote from Michael Stewart's *The Jekyll & Hyde Years*. 'On each occasion, it is the loss of office which has acted on the governing party like Dr. Jekyll's drug. Having pursued, during its last two or three years in office, essentially virtuous and responsible policies,

* *Politics and Industry – The Great Mismatch.* March, 1979.

138

now in the wilderness of opposition, it becomes a Mr. Hyde – irresponsible, wild, savaging what it previously held dear. This Hyde-like phase unfortunately outlasts the party's period in Opposition, continuing to influence its activities for the first year or two after it has again become the government. Only then does another dose of the drug lead to the responsible Dr. Jekyll reassuming control.'

This is a colourful version of the wild ideological swings in economic policy as Labour and the Tories took turns in misgoverning the country. Keynesian demand management also enabled governments to manipulate the economic time scale so that it coincided with the political one. That is, governments facing re-election tried to buy votes with give-away budgets at great cost to the economy. The report also recalled Sam Brittan's suggestion that in the sixties the government simply responded like a Pavlovian dog to the two danger signals of rising unemployment or a fall in the value of sterling by diametrically-opposed economic policies.

The range of government intervention is terribly wide, and the committee which wrote the Hansard report investigated the consequences of change in investment incentive schemes, regional policy, indirect taxation, corporation tax, and prices and incomes policy. It concluded that industry could not grow steadily when industrial policy three years from now could be in the hands of politicians of utterly opposed political views. Continued change created uncertainty which could lead to the postponement of reduction of investment projects. They could ruin a project and in some cases the whole firm, and create opportunities for foreign competitors.

An obvious example was the domestic appliance industry. According to Hoover Ltd., tight credit controls and punitive purchase tax reduced the washing machine market from more than one million units a year in the early sixties to less than 700,000 by the end of the decade. As a consequence, British manufacturing costs rapidly rose above those of foreign competitors, the industry could not afford to invest in new production capacities and when the change of government policy in 1971 allowed the long pent-up demand to explode it could only be met by imports, which rose from 8 to 18 percent in one year. With the steady reduction of purchase tax and its replacement by a more equitable single-rate VAT, Hoover did what was expected of it in a market economy. For the first time in many years investment was planned on an aggressive scale and expansion plans costing £30 million were announced. Alas, Heath's dash for freedom failed, stringent hire-purchase controls were reimposed in December 1973 and a special VAT rate of 25 percent was slapped on electrical appliances. That was the end of expansion, but imports continued to rise because foreign competitors who were free of government intervention were able to introduce more sophisticated models and reduce costs with long production runs. They have since captured the lion's share of the market.

This was only one of the cases investigated, and the report concluded that Parliament must accept a large measure of the blame for poor productivity. 'The committee fully recognized that the practice of adversary politics is deeply embedded in British constitutional convention; we concluded, however, that this practice is now producing increasingly pernicious effects so far as industry is concerned. The election manifesto, conceived in an aggressively partisan spirit, has come to be seen as committing parties more and more to legislation early in a term of office, almost regardless of the possibility that views might be changed by contact with the reality of administration and the experience of civil servants.

'The tendency to legislate in a hurry, accentuated by understandable desires to avoid the perils of an election period, all too often produces laws which, because they are evidently in need of amendment, readily fall victim to the root-and-branch repealing instinct of a triumphant opposition: and so the cycle is perpetuated, to the detriment of long-term thinking and planning. Such blatant adversary politics in time contributes to the misunderstanding of politicians by businessmen, who easily develop a contempt for the apparent instability of Westminster politics, and themselves fall into stereotyped attitudes in response. Furthermore, the problem becomes steadily more acute as the field of government activity is progressively widened, so that each shift of policy affects more and more interests.'

The committee recommended that much could and should be done by governments in the way of consultation and the giving of early notice before changes of policy affecting industry. Green and White Papers, drafted in clear every-day language, should be published early and followed by genuine discussions with industry. Arrangements made before a policy is changed by legislation should be honoured. Careful consideration should be given to the time scale within which a given initiative can be expected to bear fruit. Greater awareness of practical restraints on policy in this respect would probably lead to a reduction in the frequency with which new developments were introduced. A further and very desirable consequence would be the growth of a fuller recognition of the limitations of government intervention.

The development of the committee system in the House of Commons was recommended in order to enhance the use of expertise when legislation affecting industry was under consideration. A consensus approach was urged. Politicians of all three parties should reach agreement on significant aspects of industrial policy. The opposition parties should be represented on the National Economic Development Council, a step which would help to acquaint the alternative government with the problems of administration as they affect industry. Proportional representation should be considered because such a system, by tending to produce governments of the centre rather than either political extreme, would aid consensus on industrial and economic policy. Parliamentary reform was also necessary because no formula aimed at improving the present unhappy effect of government policy on industrial investment lead times would be more than a palliative without it.

EIGHT

The Brits, For Better or For Worse

In 1941 George Orwell wrote a short book entitled *The Lion and the Unicorn: Socialism and the English Genius*. He got the socialist bit wrong but otherwise his portraits of the British people were extraordinarily lifelike. I can remember reading it as a young soldier and seeing me and my mates in its pages. I pondered its meaning until I lost my copy somewhere in Southeast Asia, in Singapore I think. I bought another copy many years later in Washington, and was struck again by the many resemblances. It has been an incomparable reference for this enquiry.

Orwell was in love with Britain, or England as he preferred to call it, despite the poverty and misery he had observed on the road to Wigan Pier and the snobbery and privilege of the moneyed classes. He was even fairly kind to them. They had long ceased to be justifiable, and should go, but he thought that they were morally fairly sound. At least they were ready enough to get themselves killed fighting for Britain. He only despised the left-wing intelligentsia. They were severed from the common culture of the country. They took their cookery from Paris and their opinions from Moscow, and in the general patriotism of the country they formed a sort of island of dissident thought. They were ashamed of their country; they chipped away at English morale and tried to spread an outlook that was sometimes squashily pacifist, sometimes violently pro-Russian, but always anti-British. For Orwell, they were purely negative creatures, mere anti-Blimps, a by-product of ruling-class stupidity. Society could not use them, and they had not got it in them to see that devotion to one's country implied 'for better, for worse'.

As Orwell saw it, Britain was not so much divided by class as by the Colonel Blimps and the anti-Blimps, or intellectuals. Both took for granted the divorce between patriotism and intelligence. If you were an intellectual you sniggered at the Union Jack and regarded physical courage as barbarous, but the Bloomsbury highbrow, with his mechanical snigger, was as out-of-date as the Blimpish cavalry colonel. A modern nation could not afford either of them. Patriotism and intelligence would have to come together again, and Orwell thought that the war might make it possible.

It is easy to see why the intellectual left disliked Orwell, and still does. The author of *Down and out in Paris and London* could not accept their lack of patriotism. For him, Britain was different. It was not Shakespeare's sceptred isle, but when you came back from a foreign country you immediately had the sensation of breathing a different air. Small things conspired to give you this feeling. The beer was bitterer, the coins heavier, the grass greener, the advertisements more blatant. The crowds in the big towns, with their mild knobby faces, their bad teeth and gentle manners were different from a European crowd. British civilization was distinctive and recognizable, as individual as that of Spain. Moreover it was continuous, it stretched into the future and the past. There was something in it that persisted, as in a living creature.

Orwell admitted that national characteristics were hard to pin down, but nevertheless had a go. The British were not artistically gifted or intellectual. They had a horror of abstract thought, and felt no need for any philosophy or systematic world view. This was not because they were practical, as they were fond of claiming for themselves. They cared little about mere efficiency, but they had a certain power of acting without taking thought. In moments of supreme crisis the whole nation could suddenly draw together and act upon a species of instinct, really a code of conduct which was understood by almost everyone although never formulated.

Another thing one noticed when returning from abroad was the English love of flowers, which was linked to the privateness of English life. We were also a nation of stamp collectors, pigeon fanciers, amateur carpenters, darts players and crossword-puzzle fans. All the culture that was most truly native centred round things which even when communal were not official – the pub, the football match, the back garden and the 'nice cup of tea'. The liberty of the individual was still believed in, almost as in the nineteenth century. This had nothing to do with economic liberty, the right to exploit others for profit. It was the liberty to have a home of your own, to do what you liked in your spare time. The most hateful of names was Nosey Parker.

The genuinely popular culture of Britain was something that went on beneath the surface, to some extent against the existing order, unofficially, and more or less frowned on by the authorities. The common people, especially in the big towns, were not puritanical. They were inveterate gamblers, drank as much beer as their wages would permit, were devoted to bawdy jokes, and used probably the foulest language in the world. They were without definite religious belief, and had been so for centuries. Yet they had retained a deep tinge of Christian feeling, while almost forgetting the name of Christ. British civilization was also gentle. Bus conductors were good tempered and the policemen carried no revolvers. They hated war and militarism; this was deeply rooted in their history despite imperial expansion.

Another all-important British trait, according to Orwell, was respect for constitutionalism and legality, the belief in the law as something above the state and the individual, something which was cruel and stupid but incorruptible. Concepts such as justice, liberty and objective truth were still believed in. They might be illusions, but they were powerful illusions. The belief in them influenced conduct, and national life was different because of them. There was one law for the rich and another for the poor, but even the hanging judge, whom nothing short of dynamite would ever teach what century he was living in, would at any rate interpret the law according to the books and would in no circumstances take a money bribe. He was a symbol of reality and illusion, democracy and privilege, humbug and decency, the subtle network of compromises, by which the nation kept itself in its familiar shape.

Forty years on, despite the immense social change which Orwell anticipated, his Brits were still recognizable. Some bus conductors were less good humoured, and a few policemen carried guns, hangings had been abolished but flying pickets were violent. Britain was, nevertheless, still largely a gentle and ordered society. Orwell did not explain why, but emigration provides some clues. Much of the history of the world can be explained by migration – the first immigrants to arrive in America came across the Bering Strait about 20,000 years ago – but emigration from Britain was unique.

It began long before the Home Office began to keep statistics, but it is generally accepted that since the sixteenth century more than 20m Britons left these shores to start a new life abroad. There was no tribal movement; unlike those first arrivals in America they were not escaping the thrust of powerful invaders. They did not flee from tyranny or, except for the Irish, from starvation. In the early years many, to use the phrase of the American historian, Carl Bridenbaugh, were vexed and troubled Englishmen who did not like or understand the changes which were then transforming England. It is known that between 1590 and 1642 some 80,000, or two percent of the population, forsook homes and homeland. About 250,000 left in the seventeenth century, and more than 1,500,000 in the eighteenth. Between the first Reform Bill and the first world war more than 16 million sailed away to settle overseas, most of them in the United States, Canada, Australia, New Zealand and South Africa, and emigration still continues.

Conditions aboard the early trans-Atlantic ships were horrible.

The mysteries of the deep, together with the vagaries of storms and calms over a period of weeks or months, lay ahead of all vessels. For many, man-made hardships were added to the caprice of nature. The brutalities of shipmasters, the appearance of pirates and privateers, and shortages of water and food turned emigrant ships into floating islands of despair; disease and pestilence, always a grim possibility that was all too often nurtured by overcrowding, turned them into floating lazar-houses. Given favourable conditions, the voyage lasted for eight to ten weeks in 1729 and six to eight weeks in 1847. Provisions were always bad and in short supply, and towards the end of a long voyage were reduced to starvation levels. In 1729 there were only 25 biscuits left aboard one ship when land was eventually sighted.

Over-crowding was prevalent even after an Act of 1828 limited the number of passengers to be carried. A Cork merchant said that the law permitted the carrying of one passenger to every 20½ square inches of deck space, and commented that there was nothing in the annals of the slave trade to equal it. In 1729, *The Belfast News Letter* referred without apparent surprise to one emigrant ship in which an average of twelve people occupied every seven berths, each of which measured five feet ten inches long and eighteen inches wide. Headroom for the berths was less than three feet.*

I have given some detail of these coffin boats as a reminder of the toughness and adventurousness of our forbears, not only the Ulster-Scots but the British and Irish generally. The vast majority were of course working class, and they performed the most daring and portentous act in modern history by founding new nations all over the world. Nothing quite like it has happened before or since. Royal governors were appointed in some of the American colonies, but it was ordinary working-class people who poured through the Cumberland Gap to push the frontier back. It was Daniel Boone, the lone hunter, and not a military expedition, who first penetrated the West as far as the Yellowstone river.

These extraordinary deeds and achievements have been rarely acknowledged, probably because history is written by middle-class academics. American historians have been less superior, but even the Hollywood western has concentrated on a brief period after the Civil War when the West had already been won by the descendants of those vexed and troubled Englishmen. The television series, *Roots*, made much of the conditions aboard the slave ships, but as far as I know those early coffin boats, which apart from the chains were no better than the slavers, have never

* *Ulster Emigration to Colonial America, 1718–1785*. R. J. Dickson. Routledge & Kegan Paul, London. 1966

been portrayed. Little has been written or filmed about the adventures of the early British settlers in Australasia and Canada. The BBC television series on the British Empire largely ignored them. In thirteen hours of prime time not once was there a hint that much of the empire was a proletarian phenomenon, the first working-class empire in history.

The American, Australian, Canadian, New Zealand and South African accents did not come from Oxbridge or even minor public schools. The posh folk at Government House might have been nostalgic for dreaming spires and country houses, but the real pioneers remembered the stews of London, Glasgow and Belfast. They took their prejudices with them, as well as their strengths and experiences. The highlander who lost his croft in the clearances felt no compunction when taking land from the natives of his new land. The stern Protestantism of Ulster established the Bible Belt across the upper tier of southern states because at one period all the immigrants to the Carolinas came from Northern Ireland. The seed of the distinctive Australian race is from militant working-class stock. One might even trace it back to Kipling's Saxon peasant standing up to the Norman lord. Too fanciful? Not for British working-class families who pass on the story, perhaps apocryphal, of the distant relative landing at Botany Bay and asking a redcoat if there was a government in the colony. When told that there was, he said, 'Well, I'm agin it.'

For the historian, this dispersal of the British working class was largely seen only as a safety valve that helped ensure the relatively peaceful course of the country's political evolution. Britain might well have been overwhelmed by revolution without it. Emigration does not of course wholly explain the gentle nature of British civilization. There are other factors, but emigration, or rather its triumphal result, helps to reveal the nature of the ordinary Britons when not burdened and inhibited by the class, social, professional and monarchical systems which in the past condemned the vast majority to the nether world of the peasant and proletariat.

I can remember warming to the cocky self-confidence of the first Australians, Canadians and Americans I met during the early years of the second world war. I felt that they were my own kind, but one middle-class critic said that the Americans were over-paid, over-sexed and over here. I still cannot understand why he and others of his class complained about the hundreds of thousands of overseas English-speaking people coming to fight the common enemy, and to die as tens of thousands of them did. Had that critic not been so defensively class conscious he might well have wondered why those youngsters were well paid, why they had an easy relationship with their officers, and why they performed as well on the battlefield as in bed.

This snobbery was everywhere apparent, not least in the cinema. The heroes of most American war movies were sergeants or enlisted men, while in British films they were invariably officers played by actors with plummy voices which separated them from the men, who in turn were officially labelled as other ranks. The snobbish also sneered at the accent of dominion troops, but could hardly deny that British emigrants had created new worlds, new sources of wealth and new dimensions of human freedom and happiness.

Yet for all their achievements the majority remained populists. There is an old saying that scratch an American and you will find a populist even when he wears a Brooks Brothers suit, and this is largely true of most overseas English-speaking people although one can argue about the definition of populism. The Fontana Dictionary defines it as 'the promotion of political ends independently of existing parties and institutions by appealing to people, to exercise direct pressure on governments . . . populism identifies the will of the people with morality and justice, puts this "will" above all other social standards and mechanisms, and insists on a direct relationship between people and government. It is usually accompanied by a simple belief in the virtues of the people, which are contrasted with the corrupt character of the degenerate ruling class or of any dominant political or economic position or social status. Populism also tends to see conspiracy and manipulation by such groups as directed against "the people", a tendency which can be powerfully reinforced by racial or ethnic hostility'.

That, if you like, is the authorized definition of populism, and it depends heavily upon the writings of Richard Hofstadter, the American historian. Hofstadter dismissed populism as a xenophobic, simplistic, paranoid precursor of the quasi-totalitarian right of the 1950s, and suggested that it produced McCarthyism.

It did nothing of the sort. Admittedly the prairie populists of the late nineteenth century also came from McCarthy's Middle West, but so did the Progressive movement of La Follette and the liberalism of Hubert Humphrey. The populists were strong in some of the southern states which produced Governor Wallace, but after the Civil War they rightly felt that their interests were ignored and damaged by the big plantation owners and some tried to strike a common accord with the newly liberated blacks. They failed and populists became figures of fun, but they were the ur-Americans, and largely of British stock. They invented the

147

Protestant work ethic and the Horatio Alger tradition. They gave American politics its fundamental egalitarianism and American society its easy equality. They were the United States until the tidal waves of immigration from eastern and southern Europe once again changed the face of America.

This explained the xenophobia of their party, the People's party, which opposed unlimited immigration, but the Omaha platform of 1892 was not the work of intolerant, simplistic or paranoid demagogy. It called for graduated income tax, the Australian or secret ballot and other reforms which were eventually adopted by the Democratic party. Indeed, the absorption of the populists and their platform was as important as the subsequent Roosevelt coalition in transforming the Democrats into a modern liberal party.

The populists were the true descendants of the old English dissenters and levellers. They were not socialists, as some historians would have it, and they wanted to level up rather than down. They envisaged a middle-class America without the very rich and very poor. Maladjusted wealth and economic competition were seen as twin evils, and they believed that economic reform would bring about a fraternal society in which each would be for all and all for each. This idealism was evident in the Omaha platform, which announced that 'this Republic can endure as a free government only when built upon the love of the whole people for each other and for the nation'.

They spoke out for individual freedom, sought new institutions to preserve old values and dreamed of a just and egalitarian society. This was the spirit of populism, and it was our greatest export from the time the first emigrants sailed away to seek a new world and live under a rule of law based on the consent of the people. I suggest that it is still very much alive in Britain today. You do not have to scratch an American to find a populist. They can be found under the skins of many Labour and Liberal voters, and some Tories.

Populism has its dark side. Hofstadter was right when he wrote: 'if the people were to rule, if they aspired to get along with as little leadership as possible from the educated and propertied classes, whence would their guidance come? The answer was that it could be generated from within. As popular democracy gained strength and confidence, it reinforced the widespread belief in the superiority of inborn, intuitive, folkish wisdom over the cultivated, over-sophisticated and self-interested knowledge of the *literati* and the well-to-do. Just as the evangelicals repudiated a learned religion and a formally constituted clergy in favour of the heart and direct access to God, so did the advocates of egalitarian politics propose to dispense with trained leadership in favour of the native practical sense of the ordinary man with its direct access to truth.'

This has led to anti-intellectualism, and spasms of mean-spiritedness, intolerance and xenophobia in most English-speaking countries. In Britain, it helps to explain, for instance, the strengths and weaknesses of the trade union movement: the generous spirit of all for one and one for all, the whining of Mr. Alan Fisher, the general secretary of the National Union of Public Employees, whose members left the sick unattended and the dead unburied, the general resistance to change and the reluctance to see the economy in terms other than jobs, wages and security. Populism also helps to explain both the stability and inertia of whole sections of British society. In nautical language, it is the heavy ballast that keeps the ship of state on an even keel in the heaviest of weather but prevents it from catching fair breezes.

*

Orwell thought that one of the most important developments in Britain since the first world war was the upward and downward extension of the middle class which had made the old classification of society into capitalists, proletarians and small property owners almost obsolete. Property and financial power were concentrated in very few hands. Few people owned anything except clothes, furniture and possibly a house. The peasantry had long since disappeared, the independent shopkeeper was being destroyed and the small businessman was diminishing in numbers, but modern industry was so complicated that it could not get along without great numbers of highly-paid managers, salesmen, engineers, chemists and technicians of all kinds, who in turn called into being a professional class of doctors, lawyers, teachers, artists, etc., etc. In other words, the tendency of advanced capitalism had been to enlarge the middle class and not to wipe it out as it once seemed likely to do.

Much more important, Orwell continued, was the spread of middle-class ideas and habits among the working class, who were better off in almost all ways than they were before the first world war. This was partly due to the trade unions, but mainly to the mere advance of physical science. However unjustly society was organized, certain technical advances were bound to benefit the whole community because certain kinds of goods were necessarily held in common. Nearly all citizens of civilized countries enjoyed the use of good roads, germ-free water, police protection, free libraries and free education of a kind. The rich and poor read the same books, saw the same films and listened to the same radio programmes. (And, more importantly, television which was developed after Orwell's death.)

Differences had also been diminished by the mass production of cheap clothes and improvement in housing. The clothes of the rich and poor differed less. The modern council house, with its bathroom and electric light, was smaller than the stockbroker's villa, but it was recognizably the same kind of house. The effect of all this was a general softening of manners. In tastes, habits, manners and outlook, the working class and the middle class were drawing together. The unjust distinctions remained, but the real differences were diminished. The old-style proletarians – collarless, unshaven and with muscles warped by heavy labour – were decreasing in numbers, and after 1918 there began to appear something that had never existed in England before: people of indeterminate social class.

What Orwell described as the advance of physical science has continued to raise living standards, and at a rate faster than he could have anticipated. The 1980 edition of *Social Trends** showed how living standards of the majority actually rose as the nation's fortunes declined. 'Moving into the seventies we experienced inflation, relatively high unemployment and oil crises. But this last decade also saw a moderate increase in material wellbeing, a greater choice in personal consumption, the growth of the leisure industry, increases in company perks, a modest decline in the extent of inequalities in income and wealth, and a change in the balance between privately and publicly provided services.'

Political decisions and trade union clout brought about some of this progress, but the advance of physical science was responsible for the greater differences between living standards in the forties and seventies. More than half of the population lived in their own houses and also enjoyed central heating and the use of a car. More than nine out of ten had a television set and six out of ten a telephone. Two out of five spent their holidays abroad. With the exception of a few of the old industrial areas and inner cities, the average working-class family enjoyed what Orwell would have defined as a middle-class life. Indeed, forty years ago no middle-class family had a colour television set and few could afford holidays abroad – certainly not in the United States or the West Indies.

Social mobility has also increased, although it had been evident for centuries. It is worth remembering that before the French Revolution, the class structure in Britain was less rigid than in most European countries, and the pace quickened enormously after the

* Government Statistical Office, HMSO, London

industrial revolution. For instance, a study of the cotton industry, published in 1912, established that over two-thirds of the owners, directors and managers had begun their careers either as manual workers or clerks. Two American sociologists*, who quoted the study, said that the degree of social mobility in the 1950s was much the same in Britain as the United States.

Professor P. T. Bauer of the London School of Economics referred to other examples in a pamphlet on class†. Britain was supposed to be governed by a rich ruling caste but few other countries had had as many heads of government with modest beginnings. Lloyd George was a poor orphan brought up by a shoemaker uncle and Ramsay MacDonald was the illegitimate son of a fisherwoman. James Callaghan's father was a sailor and Harold Wilson, Edward Heath and Margaret Thatcher came from the lower-middle class.

The record was also good in industry. Lord Nuffield, the car manufacturer, began as a bicycle repairer. Sir John Hay, once undisputed leader of the British rubber industry, Sir John Ellerman, the shipping magnate and in his time probably the richest man in Britain, and Lord Catto, Governor of the Bank of England, came from poor families and started as clerks. Sir James Chadwick, the physicist and Master of Gonville and Caius College, Cambridge, was the son of an unskilled worker. Sir William Robertson enlisted in the army as a private in the 1880s and became Chief of the Imperial General Staff. Sir Reader Bullard, the son of a casual labourer, entered the consular service and rose to become ambassador to Iran. At a lower level of achievement, Admiral Sir Raymond Lygo, a Vice-Chief of Naval Staff, began with me as a messenger on *The Times*.

In 1977, *New Society* reported the interim findings of a major survey carried out by Dr. John Goldthorpe of Nuffield College, Oxford, and said that they proved 'Britain is a more mobile society than the received wisdom suggests: that we are a surprisingly open society, with people moving up and down the occupational escalators in a bewilderingly complex pattern. For example, only a quarter of those in social class 1 – managers and professionals – had fathers in the same category: rather less than the proportion drawn from manual working class background.' The magazine said that this was partly due to the fact that the managerial class had been expanding so fast that it simply could not recruit from among its own members, which confirmed Orwell's observation that the tendency of advanced capitalism was to enlarge the

* *Social Mobility in Industrial Society*, Seymour Martin Lipset and Reinhard Bendix. University of California Press, 1959
† *Class on the Brain*, The Centre for Policy Studies, London. 1978

middle class and create opportunity.

Goldthorpe's final report* drew a different conclusion. It in effect argued against the assumption that advanced capitalism and economic growth created a fairer society, and concluded that social reform had contributed little or nothing. The class struggle, it seemed, was the only way to break down the barriers. His findings in fact showed that what he chose to describe as the service or top class (well-paid people with career prospects in the professions, national and local government, senior management and higher technical jobs) had nearly doubled in one generation, from 13 to 25 percent of the population. They also established that nearly one-fifth had climbed upwards by means of the education system, and that the working class (manual workers) had decreased from 54 to 45 percent of the population.

Goldthorpe's methodology was criticized by some of his peers, and he did not allow for the hundreds of thousands of poor immigrants who arrived during the period under review. Had he done so, the graph of upward mobility of the native-born would have been more dramatic although probably not so much as in countries with better records of economic growth. Goldthorpe was himself a beneficiary of growth and post-war education policies. The son of a Yorkshire colliery clerk, he passed his 11-plus examination at a village school. State scholarships took him from grammar school to London University and the London School of Economics, and then to a good job at Oxford.

It would be hard to find a more typical example of upward mobility in the United States and other western democracies, and it was typical of post-war social change in Britain. Of course, the children of the powerful and the well-to-do continued to have a better start in life, as they did in other countries including the Soviet Union, but any talented boy or girl born in a slum could make it, and many of them did. The class barriers to success which were crumbling when Orwell wrote largely disappeared in the early post-war years. That was beyond dispute, but a bourgeois, or what I would prefer to describe as a modern, society did not emerge. The old class system was seen still to exist, even by those who had done well, and, real or otherwise, continued to divide the country.

One reason was the bias of sociologists, most of whom according to one of their number were 'in the main stream of left-wing ideology'. *New Society* remarked, when it reported the interim findings of Goldthorpe's survey, that the loud silence which accompanied their publication was not an isolated example of the reaction to research which did not fit easily into

* *Social Mobility and Class Structure in Modern Britain*, Oxford University Press, 1980

conventional pigeon holes. A similar silence greeted another survey which showed, contrary to the arguments of the left and the beneficiaries of the burgeoning race relations business, that West Indian children did as well, and often better, than white children in secondary schools. No wonder Orwell despised left-wing intellectuals.

Another, as I observed earlier, was that unlike Americans those who made it in Britain did not boast about their success. Instead they tended to disappear silently into the middle class and beyond without trace. They made it, but the barriers were seen to remain intact. Their silence might have been due to modesty but I suspect it was snobbery or fear of snobbery, Britain's original sin. Snobbery existed elsewhere of course, but beyond these shores was only venial. In Britain it was mortal. Tocqueville said that the British loved to have inferiors, and he could have added that this required the acceptance of superiors. One and a half centuries later snobbery continued to flourish among many social and income groups, and was nurtured by the survival of public schools. A more socially-divisive institution was difficult to imagine, but that was part of its attraction. For some Britons, to quote *My Fair Lady*, it was not what you said that was important but how you said it.

Snobbery and the idea of class were also nurtured by the Monarchy, with its supporting pyramid of princes, dukes, earls and noble lords. The Monarchy had been reduced to a constitutional cypher, and the aristocracy enjoyed few tangible privileges apart from those who had inherited a seat in the House of Lords. In one respect they were under-privileged; unlike Welsh orphans and illegitimate sons of Scottish fisherwomen, they could no longer hope to become Prime Minister. Death duties had also diminished their wealth, and many of the great country houses could only be maintained by opening them to tourists for a few bob. Some titled owners had become showmen, providing safari parks as well as old masters for the entertainment of the *hoi polloi*.

Certainly they were no cause for revolution. The Queen was safe in Buckingham Palace, although the royal family could have been advised to represent modern Britain and not the old social ideal of the land-owning gentry preoccupied with field sports. As a citizen, Princess Anne was entitled to have a jockey husband, but as a taxpayer I resented having to pay for the extension of his stables. They served no public purpose except to encourage the snobbery of pony clubs. That was probably inverted snobbery on my part. It was certainly a minority view, such was the general respect for the Queen, but it had to be accepted that the Monarchy and its supporting aristocracy perpetuated the illusion of a rigid class system.

A leading Labour politician of the centre right, a former member of more than one Cabinet, was convinced that it was not an illusion. He agreed that Britain was an open society, but too many elites and groups continued to exert undue influence. You had only to cross the park to the Athenaeum Club to see one of them, he said. There were elite groups in the Civil Service and in the City, although that was changing slowly. There was another group round the Queen who had influence. He hastened to add that he respected and liked the Queen, but the influence was there.

I recalled that I had lunch one day at the Athenaeum with a barrister and discovered that he had also been born in the East End, in a house worse than my birthplace, a back-to-back near Petticoat Lane. He remarked that if East End old boys had a club tie it would be seen more often than public school ties. I had in fact designed such a tie – red with a diagonal line repeating the old Cockney rallying cry, *Muck 'em All* – but doubted that it would be much worn when the old boys graduated.

I suggested to the politician that while some elite groups did wield undue influence some of their members had come up from below. He accepted that, but added that he had always felt an outsider even when he was in power. He allowed that similar elite groups existed in other democratic countries. They were to be found in the United States but were not so influential there because of countervailing groups, such as the baronial fiefdoms in Texas and other rich states. America was too big to be dominated by a few elites and the federal system diffused power, but Britain was a small country and all power was concentrated in London. That was why the elites were influential.

*

Margaret Thatcher proved the point when she formed her Cabinet in 1979. The lower-middle class Prime Minister who had reached the top despite residual sex discrimination was an outstanding example of the openness of British society, but apart from Peter Walker and herself the remaining 19 members were public-school men. Sixteen of them were from Oxbridge, Thatcher was the seventeenth, and three others went straight from public school into the armed services. Five had served in the Brigade of Guards and two in the cavalry. Six were Old Etonians, three were peers and another three baronets or knights. Her government, including ministers of non-Cabinet rank, had 15 peers, or the equivalent of half an infantry platoon.

Peregrine Worsthorne wrote in *The Sunday Telegraph* at the time that the Cabinet was full of hereditary peers, self-made and hereditary millionaires and wealthy landowners. Most of them had made, married or inherited splendid fortunes. He added that in recent years Tory rhetoric has suggested that socialism and egalitarianism had destroyed the old order beyond repair, but this was not quite the picture presented by the new government. Perhaps Thatcher loved a lord, like so many of her countrymen and women, but if she did not it would have been difficult, perhaps impossible, for her to form a Tory government representative of the openness of British society. In other words, the leading members of the Tory party belonged to a self-perpetuating elite. Even Edward Heath, who had looked for technocrats when he formed the 1970 Tory government, had to chose largely from former Guards officers and public-school men, and bankers, barristers and stockbrokers.

Sir Keith Joseph, who had served in both governments, was a baronet, an Old Harrovian, had read law at Oxford and was a very wealthy man. I met him in his office at the Department of Industry in Victoria Street one morning, and he was a reminder that stereotypes are often misleading. He was the son of a wealthy Jewish family, more typical of the continental bourgeoisie than British land-owning aristocrats. They had made their money in the construction and property business, and were cultivated and philanthropic. Joseph served with the gunners, and not the Guards, during the war and was wounded in Italy. He returned to Oxford after demobilization as a Fellow of All Souls, but decided that he was not a scholar and abandoned his thesis on tolerance to join the family business. He was elected Member for Leeds, North-East, in 1956.

In those days Joseph was an enlightened Tory, typical of the immediate post-war generation, and accepted Butskellism. He ascended the middle rungs of the promotional ladder fairly rapidly, and was appointed Secretary of State for Social Services in 1970. He accepted the principle of government intervention and was a big departmental spender, but publicly repented the error of statism after the Tory defeat in 1974 and took time out from active party politics to found the Centre for Policy Studies. One reason was his Victorian passion for political and moral instruction but the larger objective was to rethink Tory policies.

He quickly emerged as that rare creature in Britain, a genuine doctrinaire. As such he was a figure of fun for some people but he greatly influenced Margaret Thatcher's economic thinking. He advocated the principles of monetarism and a free economy, and his libertarianism became more passionate. His concept of an ideal society was one in which the government confined itself to making general laws within which individuals would be free to pursue their own interests, acquire property and, an important proviso often forgotten by his critics, help those who could not help themselves.

Joseph was a tense man, and it showed in his face. The customary pallor could quickly change when under tension. Perspiration appeared on his upper lip and his forehead throbbed alarmingly. His detractors called him the mad monk, which seemed not too unkind when he lectured fringe meetings at the annual party conferences. Nevertheless, he was honest enough with himself to recognize that he would make an unlikely Prime Minister and supported Thatcher's campaign for the leadership. He also had a nice wit, and when relaxed could be entertainingly provocative. His quick mind would flit from one aspect or problem of organized society to another, often appearing to change direction in mid-stream but invariably holding to a certain logic.

He was relaxed when I met him that Monday morning, and after ordering tea and biscuits agreed that the economy was not alone responsible for our decline. When allowed to, the economy would, more or less, sooner or later, improve itself. We had some of the best companies in the world and bags of talent, but a change of attitudes was needed and this would not come until the intellectuals moved away from statism. We had lived our lives too long under the complacent views of the Webbs and their staggering achievements, the London School of Economics, *The New Statesman* and the Fabian Society. There were no counter-Webbs, and the faltering of national self-confidence was due to the statist assumptions of the Labour party. The Tories were in part responsible because they had been morally browbeaten by statism, and failed to resist.

Britain was still a land of opportunity for merit and effort. Even Goldthorpe had discovered that we had a very mobile society, with an infinite number of snakes and ladders, but the intellectuals had decided we were a class-ridden society. To the extent that a class war was fought in this country, against managers and the profit motive, the class warriors had hurt the people they purported to serve. The people were poorer and less fully employed because of their efforts, and there were intangible losses such as self-respect, patriotism and values. The intellectuals had said that we must not impose standards, especially bourgeois standards which helped men and women, no matter their accent, income and background, to think in terms of months and not days. As a consequence there was a proletarian demand for immediate self-satisfaction, of spending without thinking where it came from.

156

Marx would have been surprised. About 130 years ago he had written to his friend Engels despairing of revolution in the country. 'With their bourgeois aristocracy, and their bourgeois working class, in this most bourgeois of countries how can we ever get a revolution?' He might also have been horrified, Joseph added. The 19th century was not a golden age, but the general desire for self-improvement, expressed by the workers' education movement, the trade unions, friendly societies, co-ops and the like, was a golden promise for the future. It had not been fulfilled because of statism, and it would remain unfulfilled until self-improvement was revived, education improved and embourgeoisement allowed to develop. It was not for him to decide what was a desirable state of life, but we had to stop yearning for Utopia and accept that the bourgeois society with its scope for individual choice was the least bad yet invented.

Lever and Joseph, one a socialist and the other a Tory, were the only men I met during the course of this enquiry who favoured a bourgeois society. That might have been because they were sons of Jewish immigrants. A long history of anti-Semitism and repression had conditioned many to take advantage of opportunities available in bourgeois societies, but not all. Some of the Jewish immigrants to this country in the late 19th century were socialists and anarchists. They fathered many of the intellectuals who Joseph believed had led the Labour party and the country astray, but no other ethnic or religious group was more socially mobile. They had made an extraordinary contribution to the life of Britain.

Lever's concept of what British society should be was different from Joseph's. He would not drastically reduce the power of the state as Joseph wanted to do, and arguably such drastic measures were unnecessary. West Germany was a good example of a well-run modern society; its government was decentralized but was hardly withering away, and its social services were in many ways better than those in Britain. Certainly it took better care of its old people. But both of them believed in individual effort and opportunity, the creation of wealth and the country living within its means.

Not surprisingly, I had decided as this enquiry progressed that these were the minimum requirements if the national decline was to be reversed. I pondered some other conclusions as I walked from Joseph's department to Westminster and Whitehall for another interview. The prime requirement was to improve the representation of the majority, whose basic common sense I had always assumed and which was proved time and time again by public opinion polls. It would need a change of attitudes to sweep

157

away the remnants of class and privilege and end the class war propagated by the left wing. It would require a Bill of Rights, the end of parliamentary supremacy and the replacement of the House of Lords by an elected second chamber. Trade union reform and the abolition of the Labour party's Clause Four, which gave its left-wing's demands for state socialism a certain legitimacy, were long, long overdue.

Apart from the internal affairs of the Labour party, such changes were unlikely without proportional representation and even if David Steel persuaded one of the big parties to accept PR I doubted that all the other requirements for a modern society would soon follow. We were an old country reluctant to change our ways, and the reluctance was as much evident in the trade union movement and working men's clubs as in boardrooms and Boodle's and White's.

Orwell said that an all-important English trait was respect for constitutionalism and legality. That was true to the extent that we were law-abiding, but we had refused to accept constitutional limitations as understood in other western democracies. Hence the absence of a written constitution, the supremacy of Parliament, and trade union immunities which placed both above the law. Hence the endemic volatility, the frequent change of government direction and industrial indiscipline which had combined to generate a continuing cultural revolution almost as damaging as the one which once had wracked China. Until recently we had even been reluctant to define, and thereby limit, British nationality.

The price Britain had to pay for this was an influx of about 2m West Indian and Asian immigrants, most of whom were generally unwelcomed. The immigrants were not to be blamed. As those who had come before them, they were rightly seeking a better life for themselves and their children. My grandfathers came from France and Germany, and in the East End of London where I grew up the local Cockney aborigines were almost overwhelmed by Irish Catholic immigrants and Jews from eastern Europe. We managed to live more or less peacefully alongside each other, but rarely mixing even in school, because of the good sense of all concerned. And although the Orthodox Jews looked frighteningly forbidding at times, their culture was not completely alien.

It said something for the good nature of ordinary Britons that the post-war invasion of people of different cultures provoked little violence. Very few joined the National Front, as the 1979 general elections proved, and their pathetic little marches would have gone unnoticed if the Anti-Nazi League, organized by Trots, did not seek violent confrontation. Nevertheless, if Britain had had a nationality law similar to those of other countries, immigration could have been controlled and a great deal of trouble avoided.

This general reluctance to come to terms with the constitutional limitations of a modern state was in part easy to explain. Britain was not created as were the United States, the Soviet Union, India, West Germany, China or France (which had had several goes at it). The United States was created when the states, acting for the sovereign people, ratified the constitution in 1787. India and China inherited ancient civilizations, but as nation states both were post-war creations. With the United States and other countries, they came into being as a result of a conscious act, by revolution or negotiation. Britain, like Topsy, just grew. Revolution and regicide were only incidents in our history, no more important than the Reform Bill or the Taff Vale decision.

Perhaps too much can be made of our unstructured country, which is what it is despite the Monarchy and all that goes with it, but I am not so sure. For instance, in the United States the AFL-CIO developed as a countervailing force to the bosses but also as part of American society. The union leadership did not welcome the Taft-Hartley Act and other labour laws. It funded the largest lobby in Washington to fight for legal immunities, but it even accepted the so-called right-to-work laws in the several states because it was conditioned by the constitution to abide by the acts of Congress and state legislatures.

This was all the more impressive because of the violent efforts of the bosses to prevent the early trade unions from organizing their plants, but in Britain the absence of a written constitution and Bill of Rights permitted the trade union movement to develop as a kind of alternative state. It claimed the rights and privileges of feudal barons, and eventually emerged as a sovereign power unwilling to abide by those Acts of Parliament it did not like. That was why I said earlier that the trade unions were essentially a political movement in rivalry with established authority, a status it could not have achieved within the limitation of a written constitution.

I must be careful not to appear as a union basher. I objected to the lawlessness of some of the new barons and their trained bands. Many of the barons were no more than *aparatchiks*. Others, such as Scargill, were real men but their motives were suspect. Some trade unionists were highwaymen ready to hold up the country for ransom, no matter the cost. Nevertheless, I accepted the trade unions for what they were, the most powerful populist movement in history. That was their strength. It was also their weakness; hence their Luddite approach to new technologies and their

159

assumption that the national cake was big enough for ever larger slices every year. But Mrs. Thatcher was mistaken when she decided that they could be ignored. For better or for worse, and certainly largely unnoticed, we were living in the age of populism.

For me, the prospect was both exciting and daunting. It was exciting because it could be the realization of all the hopes and aspirations of ordinary Britons, from Kipling's Saxon peasant to the Levellers, the Diggers, the Chartists and all who came afterwards. Populism was only another word for democracy, not just parliamentary democracy but something wider and more fundamental, and there was no reason to believe that the ordinary people of this country could not throw up great leaders, writers, poets and all the professional men and women required to run an efficient and humane society the like of which they had only dreamed about.

They had done it before. The genius of the British race had never been confined to one section of society. Shakespeare did not have a degree in Eng. Lit.. The great navigators who sailed away to North America, the Antipodes or wherever the wind took them, were not sprigs of the nobility nor were those who sailed after them to settle distant lands. Very few of the great inventors and engineers who led the industrial revolution went to Oxbridge. Wellington said that the battle of Waterloo was won on the playing fields of Eton, but I doubted it. Orwell, who was more generous, said that the opening battles of all subsequent wars were lost there. He could have added that other great battles such as New Orleans and Gettysburg were won by descendants of plain Brits.

The prospect was nevertheless daunting because somewhere along the way this great genius was misdirected. It probably began when the products of British genius were taken over, and claimed as their own, by the then ruling classes. Unlike in the United States, the innovators rarely enjoyed the full fruits of their labours. The bright and the inspired continued to do well for themselves and their country, but the trade union movement, which claimed to represent the immediate aspirations of its members, somehow developed the worst characteristics of American populism. No other national institution had done so much to achieve social justice for the majority. It was also the prime mover in creating the Labour party, but it became the most powerful but negative force in the country because it failed to develop constructive political, social and industrial philosophies.

It demanded job security and better living standards while making difficult and often impossible the realization of these wholly worthy objectives. It failed to discipline itself by democratic means. It had no clear vision of the future, and brought

160

down three governments, two of them Labour which was supposed to represent its interests, for muddled and perhaps ignoble reasons. In 1980 it was apparently determined to bring down the fourth.

*

Mrs. Thatcher's government could be regarded as the consequence of yet another wild swing of the pendulum, which because of the hardening ideological battle lines in Parliament led to another violent change of national direction. One trade unionist in three had voted it into power, but its ministers were hardly representative of them or the electorate generally. Her policies were more extreme than any formulated since the war, and at the end of the first year the preliminary results looked ominous. I was not the only voter to feel apprehensive; the CBI, which was regarded as the industrial arm of the Tory party, took fright as many of its members were threatened with bankruptcy. It was not the best time to introduce her new economic policies, but the world trade recession and mounting oil prices did not entirely explain the high rates of interest and inflation or increasing unemployment. She also appeared to be insensitive to the misery caused.

That said, her objectives were sensible and largely the right ones. She wanted the country first to live within its means and then create sufficient wealth to pay higher wages and provide better social services. She wanted to get rid of the quasi-corporate state, and create an environment in which the British genius could flourish. She was determined to reverse the process of centralization and cut the bureaucracies down to size before it was too late. (The number of permanent secretaries in the Civil Service had increased from 34 to 41 in the twelve years before her elevation, and they earned more than she did. The proliferation of deputy secretaries had been more dramatic, from 82 to 157.) For all her belief in the wisdom of the boardroom she was also a populist in her instincts.

She had been given a convincing mandate to stop the slide down the drain, if not specifically for her economic policies. The country seemed prepared to face up to harsh reality. Workers at British Leyland did not strike when the reorganized management dismissed a communist shop steward who had done more to ruin the company than the combined competition of foreign importers. It was also allowed to point the company in what appeared to be the right direction. There were other indications that attitudes were beginning to change.

Despite those battle lines at Westminster, some kind of progress seemed possible given political give and take. The socalled Tory wets, or moderates, were more numerous than the die-hards, or radical ideologues. The internal democracy of the party could bring about some adjustments. This and more was possible, except that the TUC denied that Mrs. Thatcher had a mandate for change and was determined to prevent it. In other words, it once again challenged the lawful government of the country. The Day of Action on May 14, 1980, was a political strike whatever Len Murray said. It was intended to be a massive display of union power to force the government to reverse its policies.

It did not succeed because the overwhelming majority of the rank and file refused to take to the streets despite inflation, unemployment and cuts in social services. Some were no doubt afraid of losing their jobs, and others were cushioned against inflation by the large wage increases which fed it. But, as Arthur Scargill had long recognized, the average trade unionist would man picket lines in furtherance of an industrial dispute but not the barricades for a political purpose.

It could be very different if her second and third years led to more winters of discontent. Picket lines could become barricades as they did at Saltley. Politically-motivated militants were only awaiting the opportunity. The doom-sayers predicted political strife between the left and right, and assumed that the left or Anthony Burgess's Tucland would eventually triumph. They were not the only pessimists. Sir Denis Barnes, a former permanent secretary who had spent most of his official life in the old Ministry of Labour and its successor the Department of Employment, concluded that Britain was a tragic battlefield of blinkered unions and political parties. The unions were only occasionally conscious of the havoc they caused, and governments lurched from one expedient to another. The battle had never been resolved, and the ultimate breakdown would come during the eighties when either the political system or the unions would have to surrender.*

All this was possible, but as I came to the end of this enquiry it seemed unlikely. I was convinced that the vast majority of the British people instinctively shied away from extremes. I had met few people who knew where they were going, but a great many who believed that Britain was still great – greater than I was prepared to concede – and would pull through. Their confidence was on the whole reassuring and only occasionally alarming.

I went up to the Yorkshire coalfields, Scargill's kingdom, and down the Frickley pit to find one ray of sunshine. At the coalface I

* *Government and Trade Unions*. Heinemann Educational. London, 1980

crawled on my hands and knees through a petrified forest of hydraulically-operated supports holding up the roof a few inches above my head, and watched a coalcutting machine tear 1,000 tons of coal from the face in one sweep. White teeth smiled out of the blackness, and friendly voices welcomed me above the scream of the machine. The miners smiled sympathetically at my discomfort, and I was happy to smile back. Coal-mining, once the Cinderella of the first industrial revolution, was again a growth industry with all the benefits, material and psychological, only growth could provide.

The oil crisis was the turning point, but the opportunity was not missed as it easily could have been. The managers told me about reorganization, the investment programme, new methods of extraction and the incentive scheme. John Stones, the union delegate at the pit, was convinced that the strikes of 1972 and 1974 had ushered in the new era. Whatever the reason, and I assumed it was an amalgam of all I had heard, the National Coal Board was at last running a reasonably efficient industry. Reasonably to the extent that it rightly sacrificed some efficiency, and profits, to ensure the well-being of the miners.

I had met Stones the night before in the working men's club in South Elmsall where I was expected to down pint after pint of strong beer. It was, I suppose, a populist's heaven. Retired miners, their faces pale after a lifetime spent underground, sat against the walls, sipping their beer and watching the young ones with their wives and girl friends knocking it back, laughing or playing bingo. It was Monday and apparently a quiet night, but the barmaids did not stop pulling at the beer pumps, filling two pint pots at a time. They all exuded the good nature and friendliness of the British, which for some reason are more apparent north of Watford.

Stones was a former grammar-school boy, physically large and articulate. He had led one of the flying pickets in the early seventies, and was cautious about the incentive scheme. He admitted nevertheless that there had been no accidents directly attributable to miners cutting corners in pursuit of more pay as Scargill had forecast, and that higher wages had increased productivity. Many young men had been attracted to the industry by the high pay, and they were different from the older generation. They owned cars and wanted to buy their own homes. He was willing to believe that the comparative affluence and security would have wider consequences.

In the manager's office after my visit to the coalface it was suggested that the privately-owned car would make it easier to close down uneconomic pits. The traditional reluctance to accept closures was in part due to transport difficulties, but the miner who had a car would be more easily persuaded to work in a pit miles from home – especially when home was a bungalow or semi in an attractive housing development and not a NCB cottage at the pit.

The office was as clean and austere as a regimental orderly room. The row of silver challenge cups on the window ledge almost completed the illusion, but not quite. The manager, Don Clay, was much younger than the average adjutant and by law wholly responsible for Frickley, which employed 1,980 men, produced 948,000 tons annually and in the previous year had made an operating profit of £1m. In other words, he was a real manager. He spent more time than he might have preferred dealing with union representatives, but could still get on with the job of producing coal.

He and Jack Wood, the local area director, were proud of the mine, with its efficient ventilating and monitoring systems which had greatly improved safety standards. It was not one of the new pits. The first shaft was sunk at the turn of the century, but the four-feet seams lent themselves to modern extraction methods. They quietly boasted that most of the machines were British-made, and that their development by the NCB had led to a healthy export business. Stones agreed that the working conditions were good.

Another pack of Scotch ale was opened – we had spent the morning down the pit and I was dehydrated – and I realized that I was in a foreign country. Relations between management and the workforce were good, in part because Clay was the son of a miner, Wood's father and grandfather had been miners, and they spoke the same language as Stones. There was not a plummy accent in the room. The manager also knew as much about the job of mining as any experienced coalface worker, and although he wore a white shirt – which appeared to be the badge of management – he was down the pit at least four mornings a week. I doubted that many managers in other industries spent as much time on the shop floor, which also helped to explain why labour relations at Frickley were better than elsewhere in Britain.

I was told, and my impressions confirmed, that Yorkshire miners were an independent lot, prone to drop their picks, if such primitive implements were still used at Frickley, to defend their inalienable rights. But absenteeism was down, and I concluded tentatively that given investment, good pay, sensible management and one union for each industry, Britain could do as well as its competitors in industries less arduous than coal-mining. That was of course Mrs. Thatcher's argument.

Not that all was well in the vast domain of the National Coal

Board. The National Union of Mineworkers opposed the closure of old and unprofitable pits in south Wales although they were dangerous and hard to work because of geological faults. In pits such as Frickley coal was not touched by human hand, while in those Welsh pits it had to be dug out with picks. The union was in the slightly ridiculous and very sad position of defending working conditions that management regarded as demeaning. It was not altogether just a matter of a blinkered union hanging on to jobs. Much more was involved, including Welsh nationalism and the clannish spirit of isolated mining villages.

The NUM was highly politicized. Many of its leaders were communists, and Scargill had his own political ambitions, but it was democratically run and strikes were not called before the membership was balloted. This too was a Tory ambition. Looked at objectively, which could of course be misleading, there was no reason why other unions could not contribute to the national wealth when given the opportunity.

*

My enquiry was coming to an end, and I went back to the Foreign and Commonwealth Office where it had begun. This time the occupant of the grand office at the head of the theatrical staircase was Lord Carrington. The pictures had also been replaced, and a splendid portrait of a Rajput prince dominated the room. His aristocratic self-confidence was shared by the Foreign Secretary, which might have explained why he was now hung over the fireplace. Peter Carrington's great, great, great grandfather was christened plain Tom Smith, but the younger Pitt had given him a barony, and six generations and 1,200 acres in Buckinghamshire certainly explained the suggestion of superiority behind the friendliness.

Carrington was fond of describing himself as a Whig, a pragmatic reformer, but he was also a Tory trimmer and this and his background had made promotion easy. He went to Eton and Sandhurst, was commissioned in the Grenadier Guards and won a Military Cross at Nijmegen. He was apparently content to be a landowner after the war, but his work with the local county agricultural committee was seen to be good training for the Parliamentary Secretaryship at the Ministry of Agriculture and Fisheries. He was next a successful High Commissioner to Australia, and after his return to London became First Lord of the Admiralty and then Defence Minister in Heath's government.

He had made it largely because of his wealth and background, but he was not the upper-class twit the ready smile suggested. We met soon after his triumph in finally resolving the Rhodesian problem, which had plagued successive governments since Ian Smith had unilaterally declared the independence of that former self-governing colony. Mrs. Thatcher had been prepared to accept the Muzorewa regime which had left the whites largely in control, but not Carrington. He had the same sense of power, and the lack of it, as did Lord Home before him, and he eventually persuaded her and the black and white Rhodesian leaders to accept the Lancaster House agreement. Rhodesia became the independent Zimbabwe, with a fair chance of making a go of it, and Britain withdrew with both relief and honour. It was Carrington's personal triumph.

His views on Britain were no less realistic. We had had it easy too long. We had been basically sheltered from economic reality by the captive markets of empire, and we had not yet learned to live in a harsh world. This had been compounded by the welfare state. He wholly accepted it, but to some extent it had gone dotty as rising expectations became too high for any government to satisfy. This was why he supported Maggie Thatcher. Every other course had been tried, and if hers failed we could expect some sharp crises. If she had got it wrong we would get to the bottom quicker than by other means, but it was worth a try. The alternatives would only hasten our genteel decline, and it would become progressively less genteel, more shabby and eventually rather nasty.

Carrington spoke without emotion, and he was not being fashionably pessimistic. He could have been a master at Eton explaining the laws of mathematics. You either learned and observed them and got your sums right, or you failed your 'A' level. There was no other alternative. Presumably when he was a boy it did not matter whether he passed or failed. He could always return to those broad acres. I bridled a bit about our having had it easy too long, but nevertheless heard him out. I was also left wondering why politicians did not speak so openly about our predicament. He might have made a good Prime Minister, but unlike Tony Benn he had not given up his title.

I walked to the Palace of Westminster in a thoughtful mood. My last appointment was with James Callaghan, the former Prime Minister and the then Leader of the Opposition. I had known Jim on and off for years, and liked him. I had resented the sneers of Crossman and other Oxbridge men in the Labour party. He was not a working-class Disraeli, Gladstone or Attlee, but he had a better understanding of his party and the trade union movement than did his middle-class critics.

As I made my usual detour, whenever time permitted, through Green Park in order to stand on the little bridge across the pond to admire the Whitehall skyline, which from that viewpoint always reminded me of story-book pictures of Sinbad's Baghdad, I recalled when we met during the winter of 1968 after he had moved over from the Treasury to the Home Office. I had had a tiring but successful year covering the American presidential elections, and as a reward the office had invited me back to London for a brief visit.

Callaghan had been appointed Chancellor of the Exchequer in 1964, when back in Washington I had assumed that he would devalue the pound. His failure to do so had ruined the chances of that Labour Administration to turn the country round, and I asked him if he had been persuaded by the Treasury knights. He said that they had behaved correctly. They had presented him with two briefs, one arguing the case for devaluation and the other defending the existing exchange rate. Then why did he not devalue? He had looked across the desk with a smile that expected understanding, and said, 'You have to have a go, Lou, you have to have a go.' Hardly an intellectual argument, but I supposed that had been the response of Britons down the ages, from Agincourt to Dunkirk. I could not condemn him for it.

Security at the Palace had been increased since the death of Airey Neave, but Westminster Hall and the floor of the House of Commons were filled with tourists. I was led through the mob to behind the Speaker's chair, and when we finally reached his office another ʲ, a trim, no-nonsense but handsome woman, gave me a cup of tea. Beyond was a little kitchen, a formica job typical of perhaps millions of kitchens in semi-detached houses. It seemed incongruous in the neo-Gothic splendour of Westminster, but was for some reason rather comforting.

I was eventually shown into Callaghan's inner office, and he rose to greet me with the usual bland but friendly smile. He made a few wry jokes about the sudden transition from being Prime Minister, when everything was done for him, to slumming it as a Leader of the Opposition. He had enjoyed all the perks that go with No 10, but clearly did not resent their sudden disappearance as did at least one former PM. The easy conversation continued, but despite the smile the eyes behind his new spectacles were watchful. After a lifetime of politics, of countless hours spent in committee rooms and in Parliament, he was rarely off his guard. He refused to talk about the unions, the base of his rise in politics. They had taken too much stick, he said. That rather limited the conversation, but he remained as avuncular as ever.

The trouble was, he said, that we did not make up our minds in time as to the consequences of the loss of empire, the passing of the special relationship with the United States, and the need for a new relationship with Europe. He recalled writing to Attlee suggesting that we should join the Schuman Plan, but the then Prime Minister decided it was largely an attempt to bring about a *rapprochement* between France and West Germany. He had always been pro-American of course. The Common Market was absurd in the sense that it could not exert economic policy through the Commission while the member-countries retained their sovereignty, but he wanted closer relations with the Community in all fields. The A310 airbus was an obvious example of how we should co-operate.

He had no idea how we would get out of the present mess. It was a matter of national psychology, and cutting taxes would not help. Those who benefited from the Tory cuts did not need such an incentive because they were too interested in their work. There was a need for industrial democracy to loosen up rigidity in industry. We must get the unions and their members involved in their companies, and made to feel that they had a stake in them.

This preliminary exchange was obviously of little interest for him, but he finally spoke with quiet passion. 'I am sure that the country will recover. Our equable climate, our surroundings and the effect of the changing seasons upon us combine to make us citizens of common sense. Thirty years in the life of a nation is only the blink of an eyelid. We have good people who have been refreshed and strengthened from time to time by immigrants. My people came over from Ireland after the potato famine, and I understand that yours arrived at the turn of the century. Already the Asians are making a contribution.

'The country will find its peace of mind again. Be sure of that. It is not in permanent decline. Our character has not changed. It is just unfortunate for us to be here at this time, but it will be very different 50 years hence. That is the moral of British history. We just have to live through this period, and wish good luck to those who are trying to change it. The change will come. You can be certain of that. There will be tremendous change and because of the energy prospects, it will come much faster than either of us think.'

The sun was shining outside, I had time to spare and walked on to Westminster Bridge and looked down river in the direction of dockland where I was born. I was in a ruminative mood, and first remembered standing on the bridge early one morning after an air raid and quoting Wordsworth's lines to myself. He was damned right. Earth had not anything to show more fair, despite the Shell building. And dull would be the clot who could pass by a sight so touching in its majesty. I also remembered lying in bed when a kid listening to the ships dropping down the river, their sirens mournful through the early morning mist but beckoning me to faraway places. I then remembered the tablet on the air shaft of Rotherhithe tunnel in Shadwell's New Park commemorating the navigator and explorer, Martin Frobisher, who had also been a privateer and had got into trouble for piracy. He had sailed from that spot 400 years ago in search of a northwest passage to Cathay and India.

All the romance was behind us, which was a pity because the Brits were a romantic people and gave of their best when their imaginations were stirred. We were apparently not born to work on production lines, which was also a pity. Perhaps the new robots and micro chips would eventually release us from that bondage. The unions did not see it like that, alas. They could defend their chains to the end, but I hoped not. I then recalled an article written by Anthony Hartley* in which he quoted Lord Hugh Cecil on what the loss of empire might mean to Great Britain: Losses to a nation may be so great that they change the character of the nation itself. It would be so with us if we lost all our dominions beyond the seas. Here we shall find help in the conception of vocation which is familiar to the religious mind. We must say that national existence means the capacity to fulfil the national vocation.

The dominions beyond the sea had gone with the romanticism, and we had not found a new vocation, or a new role as Dean Acheson once said. That was partly the cause of our continued decline. The modernization of the economy was still the first priority, but it was hardly a vocation unless the objective was to build the new Jerusalem and make England a greener and pleasanter land. That vision had not been forgotten; I was certain that it was still there although the ideological battles in Parliament had slowed down the journey to the top of the hill and the bureaucracies had diminished what had been achieved.

Hartley saw a new dilemma. The government of empire, he believed, created a class of leaders and administrators formed by the exercise of responsibility and, at their best, by a concept of service to those under their rule. The question was not merely whether they could be fitted into the diminished Britain of the late twentieth century, but also whether their values of honesty, a sense of service and a respect for justice could persist. A society bent on survival by modernizing its economy was unlikely to pay too much attention to moral restraints gestated in more prosperous days, and it would be a pity if those values were to be forgotten.

His fears were unfounded. Those values were not the reward of empire, nor the exclusive property of an elite. They were part of our long history, and were shared by most Britons, including trade union leaders. The problem was how to reform Parliament and the electoral system, the Civil Service and the TUC to establish a new

* *Journal of Contemporary History, Vol 15, 1980.* Sage, London and Beverley Hills

equilibrium. Given these reforms, we could improve the economy and move with greater confidence towards a fairer and more open society. It should not be difficult, the case for each reform had long been argued, but the question was how to change attitudes. How could the fraternal and generous instincts of populism be nurtured and directed for the greater good? How could the majority be persuaded of the benefits of a truly bourgeois society?

The questions did not necessarily pose a paradox, although I did not have the answer. Instead, I sought comfort and hope in what Orwell had written when he looked into the uncharted future. 'England will still be England, an everlasting animal stretching into the future and the past, and, like all living things, having the power to change out of recognition and yet remain the same.'

Index

171

Hutton, Graham, 122

175

Plaid Cymru, 33
Polaris missiles, 11, 16, 22, 108
Pompidou, Georges, 63
Populism, 64, 147–9, 160;
    definition, 147
Powell, Enoch, 34, 54, 100, 107, 117
Prime Minister, powers of, 25–7,
    30, 36, 63
Pring, David, 36n.
Prior, James, 118, 120–2
Private Eye, 19
Profumo scandal, 109
Progressive movement (USA), 147
Proportional representation (PR),
    32–3, 36, 158
Protection of Information Bill
    (1980), 39
Public Accounts Committee, 50
Pym, Francis, 113, 118

Quangos, 8, 43

Ramsey, Bob, 92
Rees, Merlyn, 21–2, 52
Referendum: use of, 34; European,
    34
Review Committee on Overseas
    Expenditure, 15
Rhodes, William, 124–5
Rhodesia, 166
Richardson, Keith, 138
Robertson, Sir William, 151
Rodgers, William, 73
Rolls Royce, 126
Roosevelt, President Franklin D.,
    27
Rose, Paul, 28–9
Rousseau, Jean-Jacques, 88

Saltley pickets, 77, 118, 162
Scanlon, Hugh (Lord Scanlon), 90,
    91
Scargill, Arthur, 74, 77, 83–4, 89,
    159, 162, 163
Schmidt, Helmut, 32, 33
Schuman Plan, 168
Scotland, devolution, 33
Scottish Nationalist Party, 33
Sharp, Dame Evelyn, 46

Sherman, Barrie, 86–7
Shinwell, Emanuel (Lord
    Shinwell), 10
Shop stewards, 77–81, 85, 90, 161
Shore, Peter, 73
Sieff, Lord, 131–5; on human
    relations in industry, 133–5
Sked, Alan, 105n.
Slater, Jim, and Slater Walker
    Securities, 111, 127
Smith, Adam, 129
Social Contract (1974), 88
Social mobility, 150–2
Social Trends (Government
    Statistical Office), 150
Socialist Workers Party, 137
South Africa, 12, 144, 146
Soviet Union, 9, 67, 152;
    imperialism, 9; inefficiency, 45,
    70
Spaak, Paul-Henri, 13–14
Spectator, 108
Spence, Sir Basil, 15
Spoils system, 43
Statute of Artificers, 94
Steel, David, 31–2, 158
Stewart, Michael, 138
Stock Exchange, London, 127
Stokes, Lord, 135
Stones, John, 163, 164
Strafford, third Earl of, 6
Strikes, 58, 76–9
*Strikes and the Government,
    1893–1974* (Wigham), 78n., 94n.,
    95n.
Suez crisis (1956), 11, 26, 28, 67,
    105, 107, 109
Sunday Telegraph, 75, 154
Sunday Times, 91, 138
Sweden, 80
Switzerland, use of referendum,
    34

Taff Vale judgement, 95
Taft-Hartley Act, 159
Thatcher, Margaret, and Thatcher
    ministry, 16, 17, 28, 51, 61, 63, 72,
    81, 89, 104, 110, 113–19, 136, 151,
    155, 156, 161, 162, 164, 166; and